THE CHINESE JEW

by
Elaine Miller

1   EXT. DAY. WEST SIDE HIGHWAY. NEW YORK, NY. JULY, 1974.   1

Open on overhead shot of a silver colored hatch-back Chevrolet Vega automobile. It is traveling uptown on the West Side Highway. Graffiti disfigures the stonework abutting the Highway. Refuse blows across the median. The Vega exits at the 125th Street exit. It slows down in the city streets, stops at traffic lights, turns, then speeds up as the driver searches for curbside parking. Finally, the vehicle approaches a small, vacant spot located under an overpass of the Highway. Expertly, the driver backs into the spot in a single movement. Not content with having parked successfully, the driver attempts to overcorrect and bumps the vehicle in front of the Vega.

2   INT. VEHICLE. CONTINUOUS.   2

MIRIAM, a slender twenty-one year old woman, with curly, blond hair, and a snub nose, is seated behind the wheel. She is wearing a short, flowered two-piece suit, tight waisted and fastened with round, red plastic buttons.

                    MIRIAM
            Jesus Christ!

3   EXT. VEHICLE. CONTINUOUS.   3

MIRIAM exits the Vega and inspects the two cars. There is no visible damage. She grimaces. She locks the door to the Vega and takes off, her leather shoulder purse swinging with the motion. She walks past wet streets, steaming from an early morning rain, open doored bodegas and garages. She runs across Broadway, dodging cars and enters a tall building. "ASTROPHYSICS DEPARTMENT, COLUMBIA UNIVERSITY" is etched in the lintel above the double doors.

4   INT. ASTROPHYSICS BUILDING. CONTINUOUS.   4

Dark paneled lobby, half-marbled. A brass elevator call panel is fastened on the wall adjacent to the elevator door.

MIRIAM stands before the elevator door. She is daydreaming as she looks up at the half-moon metal plate listing the floors. She watches the arrow fall to the number "1".

Suddenly, the elevator door opens revealing a sole occupant. It is RANDALL.

RANDALL is twenty-three, a tall, black haired, handsome Oriental man. The overhead light shines on his hair, giving it a blue glow. He looks at MIRIAM intently.

4   CONTINUED:

MIRIAM enters the elevator. She turns to face the control panel and presses a finger against the "11" button. His hand rises above her and presses the "10" button.

>   RANDALL
>   (In a deep voice) Excuse me.

They wait in silence as the elevator climbs. Finally, MIRIAM speaks.

>   MIRIAM
>   Nice day. (MIRIAM cringes but RANDALL
>   is unaware of her gesture)

>   RANDALL
>   Do you work here?

>   MIRIAM
>   Yes.

>   RANDALL
>   Where?

>   MIRIAM
>   Professor Norton's office. It's a
>   summer job.

>   RANDALL
>   What do you do?

>   MIRIAM
>   I'm going to law school in--.

The opening of the elevator door interrupts her.

>   RANDALL
>   Nice meeting you. My name is RANDALL.

The elevator door closes.

>   MIRIAM
>   (Whispering) My name is MIRIAM.

                                                    FADE OUT:

5   INT. OFFICE. ASTROPHYSICS BUILDING. CONTINUOUS.

MIRIAM turns the doorknob and opens the glass-paneled door. Two seated women are revealed. They are BLYTHE and DELORIS. Both look up.

DELORIS
Good morning, Ms. MIRIAM. How was the traffic? I can't imagine why anyone would drive back and forth from Brooklyn every day.

MIRIAM
(Walking towards her desk, opening a drawer and placing her purse in it) Fine. (She sits down and bangs her knee on the open drawer) OW! (Shuts the drawer)

BLYTHE
You do that every time.

DELORIS
Maybe we should tape it shut. Ms. MIRIAM is an absent minded professor.

MIRIAM smiles but doesn't participate in the banter. She reaches up and removes a stack of papers from an overhead shelf. The title page of the stack reads "Proposed Orbiting Space Station Project". She begins to type. The sounds of a radio broadcast are heard in the background.

DELORIS (cont'd)
(To BLYTHE) Turn it up.

BLYTHE adjusts the volume of the radio, perched on the window sill. It is a live broadcast of the Watergate hearings being held in Washington, D.C. The three listen intently.

BLYTHE
This Sam Ervin character. I can't understand a word that he's saying.

DELORIS
Ssh. That's because you're not black.

BLYTHE
What does that mean?

DELORIS
You don't get his southern accent.

BLYTHE
Well, then how do you get it? You're from the Bronx.

5   CONTINUED: (2)   5

>   DELORIS
>   I have people down there! Will, you be
>   quiet? This is history!
>
>   BLYTHE
>   I can't believe this stuff.

MIRIAM shakes her head, amused. She continues to type.

                                                    FADE OUT:

6   EXT. DAY. OFFICE. ASTROPHYSICS BUILDING.   6

Noon that day.

MIRIAM exits the building and walks towards the campus
quadrangle. She approaches a vacant bench and sits. She
places a brown bag on her lap and removes an aluminium-
foiled sandwich. Slowly, she unfolds the wrapping as she
watches the people walking to and fro. She smiles, lost
in her own thoughts. When she finishes the sandwich she
re-folds the foil, running her finger-nail across its
edges.

>   MIRIAM
>   RAAN-DALL. (She nods) I like it.

She shrugs her shoulders as if to brush off a negative
thought. She rises and walks towards one of the grand
columned libraries. She discards the crumbled paper bag
into a refuse container. She looks up and straightens her
flowered jacket and enters the building.

7   INT. LIBRARY. COLUMBIA UNIVERSITY. CONTINUOUS.   7

MIRIAM withdraws her employee identification card and
shows it to the security guard who waves her in. She
smiles. She walks towards the stacks and begins to wander
up and down the rows, removing, examining and replacing
books. Suddenly, she looks at her wristwatch and turns to
leave. Reluctantly, she walks out of the darkened library
into the summer sun and descends the wide stone steps.

                                                    FADE OUT:

8   INT. DAY. OFFICE. ASTROPHYSICS BUILDING.   8

Next day.

MIRIAM, BLYTHE and DELORIS sit at their desks. Their
humming typewriters remain idle. They are listening to
the radio transmission of the Watergate hearings.

8   CONTINUED:

                         VOICE
               Mr. BUTTERFIELD, are you testifying
               that--

                         DELORIS
               Did you hear that? BUTTERFIELD just
               told the congressional committee that
               Nixon taped himself. Can you believe
               it? I wonder if the other people knew
               about it. Isn't it illegal to tape
               someone's conversation without their
               consent? You know, don't you MIRIAM?
               Aren't you going to law school?

                         BLYTHE
               (Laughing) Give me a break. She's not
               a lawyer yet.

                         DELORIS
               But didn't she work in a law firm?

                         MIRIAM
               I typed subpoenas.

Suddenly, there is a knock on the door. A shadow is
visible through the glass panel. The women turn. It is
RANDALL. He is wearing a red boat-neck sweater over a
white button-down shirt. His black trousers are neatly
pressed.

                         RANDALL
               Hi.

MIRIAM sits silently as BLYTHE and DENISE stare.

                         RANDALL (cont'd)
               I was wondering if you were free for
               lunch.

MIRIAM grabs her purse from the open drawer and slowly
rises. She pushes the drawer shut to avoid hitting her
knee. She walks towards RANDALL and then returns to her
desk and turns off her electric typewriter.

                         MIRIAM
               Sure.

MIRIAM walks past RANDALL into the hallway. The door
closes behind them. BLYTHE and DELORIS continue to stare.
Finally, DELORIS, raising an eyebrow, shakes her hand as
if to say "Hot!".

9   INT. HALLWAY. ASTROPHYSICS BUILDING. CONTINUOUS.   9

MIRIAM and RANDALL walk towards the elevator.

                    RANDALL
          I asked Professor Norton about you.

                    MIRIAM
          What did he say?

                    RANDALL
          He said that you were good at what you
          did.

                    MIRIAM
          (Laughing) I guess I've been cleared
          for lunch.

                                                    FADE OUT:

10   INT. RESTAURANT ATRIUM. CONTINUOUS.   10

MIRIAM and RANDALL sit at a table in a glass-enclosed
outdoor room. Occasionally, pedestrians stop and stare
into the room, shading their eyes. As more people enter
the room, the noise level rises. Lights and shadows play
on MIRIAM and RANDALL as they examine their menus. A
WAITRESS is standing next to them holding an order pad.

                    WAITRESS
          Will that be all?

                    RANDALL
          (Looking at MIRIAM) Yes. Thanks.

                    MIRIAM
          (Folding her hands) I've never been
          here before.

                    RANDALL
          Neither have I.

MIRIAM observes his broad, face and well-proportioned
body.

                    MIRIAM
          Where did you go to school?

                    RANDALL
          Brown. My parents came to the United
          States when I was twelve and settled
          in Massachusetts.

MIRIAM
Oh?

RANDALL
My dad taught at MIT. My mom is an oncologist.

MIRIAM
Oh.

RANDALL
Where are you from?

MIRIAM
Here. I was born in Brooklyn. I'm a first generation American. My parents were in the Holocaust.

RANDALL
I'm sorry.

MIRIAM
(Shrugging) They survived. I guess it made them stronger.

RANDALL
Have you ever gone out with a Chinese man before?

MIRIAM
(Laughing) I've never gone out with someone who wasn't Jewish before.

RANDALL
Why did you go out with me?

MIRIAM
You asked.

RANDALL
That's all?

MIRIAM
If you get to know me better, you'll find out that's saying alot.

RANDALL
What do you mean?

MIRIAM
You'll see.

10 CONTINUED: (2)

                    RANDALL
        I hope so.

ENTER WAITRESS carrying tray. She places sandwiches and drinks on the table. She smiles and EXITS.

                    RANDALL (cont'd)
        You don't look Jewish. You look
        Swedish.

                    MIRIAM
        (Pausing) You know, I've been hearing
        that since I was a kid. I'm never sure
        whether it's a compliment or not.

                    RANDALL
        You're right. I apologize. We're going
        to have to get over these racial
        stereotypes if we're going to be
        friends.

                    MIRIAM
        (Picking up a potato chip and waiving
        it at RANDALL) I agree. I think we're
        going to have to get off on the right
        foot. (Munching the chip) I must admit
        that I wasn't sure if you were
        Japanese or Chinese.

                    RANDALL
        (Laughing) That hurt.

                    MIRIAM
        (Smiling) As long as we get everything
        out in the open.

                                          FADE OUT:

11 EXT. RESTAURANT. CONTINUOUS.

MIRIAM and RANDALL exit the restaurant. A breeze flutters the hem of MIRIAM's skirt. She walks slowly. She looks up at the stone buildings towering above them. Many of the buildings lower facades have been blackened by years of exhaust fumes. MIRIAM and RANDALL pass a policeman standing beside an expired parking meter, retrieve his ticket book from his rear pocket, a saleswoman leaning over window display re-arranging shoes, children running, a woman carrying an orange colored toy poodle, a young man licking an ice-cream cone as chocolate sprinkles fall to the ground.

11   CONTINUED:

                    RANDALL
          Would you like to see a play?
          Shakespeare in the Park. Have you ever
          been there?

MIRIAM shakes her head.

                    RANDALL (cont'd)
          How about tonight? We'll leave
          straight from work.

MIRIAM pauses.

                    MIRIAM
          I have to make some telephone calls
          but I'm sure it wouldn't be a problem.

                    RANDALL
          Another date?

                    MIRIAM
          No. No, no. Some family business.
          Dinner. My mother expects me home. She
          gets anxious when I don't, you know,
          show up.

                    RANDALL
          (Holding the door of the Astrophysics
          Building open) We have a tight knit
          family, too. Of course, it helps that
          they live in Massachusetts.

MIRIAM smiles and enters the building.

                                                  FADE OUT:

12   INT. OFFICE. ASTROPHYSICS BUILDING. CONTINUOUS.   12

DELORIS, BLYTHE and MIRIAM are seated at their
typewriters.

                    DELORIS
          (Looking up) You're what?

                    MIRIAM
          (Reluctantly) I'm going out with him
          tonight after work.

DELORIS shuts off the radio.

                    DELORIS
          What are you going to wear?

12   CONTINUED:

DELORIS and BLYTHE look at MIRIAM expectantly.

                    MIRIAM
(Looking down at her blouse, plaid vest and short skirt) This.

                    DELORIS
I don't think so. You look like a Mary Poppins action figure that got caught in the clothes dryer. You do not wear an outfit like that to a play in Central Park with dude like that.

                    BLYTHE
She's right.

                    MIRIAM
Well, there's nothing I can do about it. I can't go back to Brooklyn to change.

                    DELORIS
(Rising) We have to do something about this. BLYTHE, get up. We're going shopping.

                    MIRIAM
(Protesting) I can't go. I just got back from lunch.

                    DELORIS
How long have you been working here?

                    MIRIAM
Three weeks.

                    DELORIS
I've been here five weeks. Technically, that makes me your senior. I say we go. We'll just run across Broadway to that boutique. I have something in mind.

                    BLYTHE
C'mon. I know the store. You'll love it.

                    MIRIAM
Well, at least leave someone a note.

12 CONTINUED: (2)

                    DELORIS
          (Standing still) Leave whom a note?
          There's no one in. They're all at a
          conference in Washington.

                    MIRIAM
          (As DELORIS and BLYTHE pull her out of
          her chair and push her out of the
          office) I don't know about this.

                                        FADE OUT:

13   INT. RETAIL STORE. CONTINUOUS.

MIRIAM stands before a tri-fold mirror in the dressing room of a clothing store. She is being observed through the open door by DELORIS, BLYTHE and a SALESWOMAN. Piles of clothing rest on the dressing room benches. MIRIAM is wearing white slacks and a white blouse. A thin gold belt circles her narrow waist. She draws herself up.

                    DELORIS
          That's it!

                    SALESWOMAN
          It's certainly very flattering.

                    BLYTHE
          (Handing MIRIAM a pair of sandals) Try
          these on.

                    DELORIS
          I wish I had your figure. No butt.
          You're built like a boy.

                    MIRIAM
          I don't know. I don't really like
          revealing clothes.

                    DELORIS
          (Interrupting) Yes, you do. (To the
          SALESWOMAN) She'll take it. Now, get
          dressed. (Closing the dressing room
          curtain with a bang)

MIRIAM stares at herself. She touches the swell of her breast visible above the shirt. Her fingers move up her neck and into her thick, curly hair. She lowers her chin and then looks up. She begins to remove her clothes.

                                        FADE OUT:

THE CHINESE JEW 12

14   EXT. SUNSET. DELACORTE THEATER. CENTRAL PARK, NY.   14

That day.

MIRIAM and RANDALL stand on line outside the amphitheater. A large crowd surrounds them. Posters announce
the performance of "'King Lear' starring James Earl
Jones". Drawings of the actor's face crowned by a metal
diadem resting low on his forehead stare down at them.
The crowd moves slowly.

                    RANDALL
          Did you call your mother?

                    MIRIAM
          Yes.

                    RANDALL
          Any problems?

                    MIRIAM
          Not at all.

                    RANDALL
          What did you tell her?

                    MIRIAM
          I just said that I wouldn't be home
          for dinner.

                    RANDALL
          That's all?

                    MIRIAM
          Yes.

                    RANDALL
          Did you tell her that you were going
          out with me?

                    MIRIAM
          No.

                    RANDALL
          Why not?

                    MIRIAM
          I don't tell my mother about my
          private life. We don't have that kind
          of relationship. I read that this play
          got great reviews. I've never seen
          King Lear. Have you?

14 CONTINUED:

                    RANDALL
          Once, in Stratford, Connecticut.

                    MIRIAM
          I've been there. The New York City
          School system had a program. Students
          were bused there for a day trip.

                    RANDALL
          What did you see?

                    MIRIAM
          I don't remember. It was a comedy.

                    RANDALL
          Did you like it?

                    MIRIAM
          Very much.

They move forward. MIRIAM looks overhead. Off in the
horizon, reams of blue light streak across the
approaching twilight. She breathes deeply and grasps the
black railing framing the walkway leading to the theater.
She turns and bumps into RANDALL.

                    MIRIAM (cont'd)
          (Laughing) Excuse me.

                    RANDALL
          I don't mind.

MIRIAM is very aware of RANDALL's presence. She notices
that other young men pass by and gaze at him with
interest.

                    RANDALL (cont'd)
          (Whispering) You look good.

                    MIRIAM
          (Blushing) Thanks.

15 INT. AMPHITHEATER. CONTINUOUS.   15

MIRIAM and RANDALL enter the amphitheater and find their
seats. Colorful banners ring the upper level of the
theater. On the stage, an elevated throne is set before a
backdrop simulating castle walls. MIRIAM and RANDALL
find their seats. He places his arm over the back of her
seat. She trembles. Several sharp trumpet blasts are

15 CONTINUED:

heard. The house lights are lowered. MIRIAM crosses her legs, expectantly.

FADE OUT:

16 INT. AMPHITHEATER. CONTINUOUS.

MIRIAM's eyes brim, her hands folded tightly as she watches the performance. The lead actor, swarms across the stage, his deep, booming voice, his precise diction, his rage, his regret, his pride, filling the theater. His royal robes skims the floorboards as he rages, his fury unrequited.

> KING LEAR
> How sharper than a serpent's tooth it is to have an ungrateful child.

MIRIAM continues to watch, mesmerized. The play ends. Explosive applause echo throughout. MIRIAM does not applaud. RANDALL waits for her to compose herself. Slowly, she rises and begins to walk towards one of the theater exit. RANDALL removes his sweater and places it on her shoulders. Shyly, she inhales his fragrance.

> MIRIAM
> (As they begin to descend the exit ramp) I never had an experience like that. He was magnificent.

EXIT MIRIAM and RANDALL.

17 EXT. CENTRAL PARK. CONTINUOUS.

MIRIAM and RANDALL stroll out of the park.

> RANDALL
> Would you like to get something to eat?

> MIRIAM
> No, I'd better be getting back. It's 10:30. Work tomorrow.

> RANDALL
> Tomorrow's the Fourth of July.

> MIRIAM
> It is?

> RANDALL
> Yes.

17   CONTINUED:

                        MIRIAM
              I forgot. Here's my car. Where do you
              live?

                        RANDALL
              Eighty-ninth and Broadway.

    They enter her Chevrolet Vega.

18   INT. MIRIAM'S CAR. CONTINUOUS.

    MIRIAM drives. RANDALL sits on the passenger side. They
    drive uptown. MIRIAM drives slowly anticipating the
    yellow traffic lights and stopping as if to prolong her
    time with RANDALL.

                        RANDALL (cont'd)
                    (Indicating an apartment building)
              Here it is.

    MIRIAM pulls into an empty parking space.

                        RANDALL (cont'd)
              Would you like to come up?

                        MIRIAM
              (Hesitating) I can't.

                        RANDALL
              I understand. Do you mind if I kiss
              you?

                        MIRIAM
              I would mind if you didn't.

    RANDALL leans over the center console and draws MIRIAM
    towards him. Firmly, he presses his lips against hers.
    She responds willingly. He moves away. Silently, he opens
    the car door. She waves and smiles weakly. She pulls out
    of the parking spot and drives away. She turns at the
    next traffic light and begins to drive south. Eighty-
    fifth Street. Eighty-fourth Street. Suddenly, she pulls
    over to the side of the road. She fumbles in her purse
    for coins. She turns off the car engine and exits the
    car, locking the door.

19   EXT. STREET. CONTINUOUS.

    MIRIAM races to a public telephone. A fluorescent light
    illuminates the interior of the telephone carrel. "TAKI
    181!" is scribbled on the cracked Plexiglas panels. She
    inserts the coins and dials.

19 CONTINUED:

> MIRIAM (cont'd)
> Hello? Hello, BLYTHE? Is that you? I'm sorry if I woke you up. Oh, it was great. BLYTHE, I need a favor. I'm going to ask you to do something weird. Got a pencil? Okay. Call my mother. You have her number, right? It's the same as mine. I'll give it to you again. Okay, that's it. Tell her that I asked you to call and that I-- um, I went to the theater and there was an electrical problem and the show started late and I'm going to be late and that I'm going to spend the night with you. Yes! But I'm not. Just tell her that I am. Give her your number but make a mistake on the last two digits. You can do it! Please. She'll buy it. BLYTHE! Thanks. Thanks. I owe you one.

MIRIAM hangs up the telephone and rushes back into her car.

20 INT. MIRIAM'S CAR. CONTINUOUS.

MIRIAM drives to the next intersection turns around and heads uptown. The streets seem to be increasingly crowded with vehicles and pedestrians, frustrating her pace.

> MIRIAM
> (Looking up at a red traffic light)
> C'mom.

Her fingers play against the steering wheel. She finds herself behind a vehicle waiting for a parking space, delaying her further. She re-enters traffic and then is stopped behind a fuming bus, delivering passengers. Finally, she drives up to RANDALL's apartment building. She finds the same spot that she had earlier parked at, unoccupied. She parks, locks her car and jumps out.

21 EXT. STREET. CONTINUOUS.

MIRIAM stops, returns to the car and kisses its roof. She racing towards the entrance of the building.

22 INT. LOBBY. RANDALL'S APARTMENT BUILDING. CONTINUOUS.

The lobby is marble walled. Highly polished fixtures gleam.

22 CONTINUED:

Enter MIRIAM, running. She slows down and approaches the uniformed doorman standing behind a counter.

> MIRIAM
> (Breathlessly) RAN-RANDALL--
>
> DOORMAN
> RANDALL CHANG?
>
> MIRIAM
> (Sheepishly) I just dropped him off.

The DOORMAN picks up a telephone receiver and dials, looking noncommittally at MIRIAM.

> DOORMAN
> Mr. CHANG? I'm sorry to disturb you. A young lady is here to see you. Miss-?
>
> MIRIAM
> MIRIAM.
>
> DOORMAN
> Ms. MIRIAM. Yes, sir. Thank you.
> (Replacing the receiver) Nine B. The elevator is to your right.
>
> MIRIAM
> Thank you.

MIRIAM walks towards the elevator doors, their patina reflecting an amber glow. She pushes the call button. She then grasps the shoulder strap of her purse with both hands and breathes deeply. The doors open. She enters. She pushes the "9" button. The doors close and the elevator motor begins to whirl. The elevator stops, the doors open and she exits. Uncertain of the direction in which to go, she turns left onto the black and white mosaic tiled hallway. Suddenly, she hears a door open. RANDALL appears. He is wearing a short, silk robe. He holds the door to his apartment open. She enters his apartment.

> MIRIAM (cont'd)
> I forgot to return your sweater.
> (Removing it from her shoulders, she hands it to him as he closes the door behind her)

FADE OUT:

23   INT. RANDALL'S APARTMENT. CONTINUOUS.   23

The apartment has gleaming parquet floors. A colorful, abstract rug lies in the center of the main room. Overhead recessed lights illuminate a teak wall unit housing a bank of steel-colored stereo equipment. City lights are visible through a series of floor to ceiling windows. Speckled granite eggs huddle together in a crystal dish resting on metallic-framed, glass topped table set before a curved, upholstered sofa. The room appears cool and clean.

MIRIAM walks towards the windows. She sighs as if the energy that had been propelling her, has expired. She walks over to the wall unit. Oversized art books are stacked horizontally. She withdraws one of the books. The title reads "Ancient Rome".

                    RANDALL
          Can I get you something?

                    MIRIAM
          No, thanks.

RANDALL walks through an open arched doorway into the kitchen. He opens the refrigerator door and pours bottled water into clear glass. He closes the refrigerator door and drinks.

                    RANDALL
          Are you sure?

                    MIRIAM
          Yes.

MIRIAM sits on the sofa and then rapidly, stands up, as if changing her mind.

RANDALL re-enters the room. His muscled chest is visible under the robe. His face, framed by broad, fine haired brows, is in repose.

                    RANDALL
          I'm glad that you came back.

                    MIRIAM
          Well--

RANDALL moves closer to her and kisses her lips. His arms encircle her back and draw her closer. MIRIAM's eyes are open as if in panic, regret, fear and passion. Her eyelids lower.

23 CONTINUED:

Shortly, they make their way into RANDALL's bedroom, a well-decorated room with brown suede wallpaper and chrome accents. They lay on the shearling coverlet, facing each other. MIRIAM's long fingers plane RANDALL's breast. She shivers as if chilled. With increasing vigor, they explore each other's bodies until she lays naked beneath him. Balancing himself on his powerful arms, he rises and descends on her willing body. She demands more and more of him until they are both exhausted.

                                        FADE OUT:

24 INT. DAY. RANDALL'S BEDROOM.   24

Sunrise.

MIRIAM and RANDALL sleep. MIRIAM lies on her back. RANDLL lies on his side, his arm around her waist.

MIRIAM's eyes fly open. She turns to look at RANDALL. She moves his arm and slips out of the bed. She enters the bathroom and gently closes the door behind her. She depresses the light switch. White, ceramic floor to ceiling tiles reflect the light. She looks at her face in the wall mirror. Her cheeks are flushed, her hair tangled. She steps in the shower and turns the porcelain knob marked "HOT". Soon, a steamy fog began to fill the room. She wraps a towel around her hair. She steps in the shower and begins to soap her legs and arms. She rinses and steps out of the shower. She takes a another towel from a rack and wraps it around her body. A thick, white robe is hanging on the back of the door. She puts it on. She rubs her cheek against the soft material and inhales, as if she recognizes his scent. She opens the bathroom door and exits the bathroom.

MIRIAM enters the kitchen. RANDALL is standing at the stove, cracking eggs.

                    MIRIAM
          (Surprised) Good morning.

                    RANDALL
          Find everything you need?

                    MIRIAM
          Yes.

                    RANDALL
          Coffee?

                    MIRIAM
          Please.

24 CONTINUED:

MIRIAM sits at the square, butcher block table surrounded by four chrome-framed, cane-backed chairs. RANDALL approaches, holding an electric percolator and fills a large mug with brewed coffee. She smiles and reaches for the ceramic cream and sugar bowls. She examines them. They are shaped like roosters. She lifts the lid of the creamer by its red comb.

          RANDALL
Scrambled eggs, okay?

          MIRIAM
Fine.

MIRIAM waits for RANDALL to seat himself at the table.

          MIRIAM (cont'd)
I'm not a morning person.

          RANDALL
You look fine to me.

They sit silently as they finish their breakfast.

          MIRIAM
(Rising) I guess I'd better be going.

          RANDALL
What do you mean? We're going to spend the day together.

          MIRIAM
(Sitting back down) Okay. But I'd better move my car.

          RANDALL
MIRIAM, it's the Fourth of July. Alternate side of the street parking is suspended.

          MIRIAM
I forgot.

          RANDALL
How long have you been driving?

          MIRIAM
Six months.

          RANDALL
That long?

24 CONTINUED: (2)

> MIRIAM
> (Interrupting) I tell you what. I need to go home. It's only about forty minutes away and there won't be any traffic today. I'll be back about one or two.

> RANDALL
> Is that what you want to do?

> MIRIAM
> I think I should. My mother is a widow and she worries. And I need to change my clothes.

RANDALL rises and walks over to MIRIAM and kisses her forehead.

EXIT RANDALL.

> RANDALL
> Hurry back.

RANDALL walks into the next room.

MIRIAM bites into her toast and smiles.

FADE OUT:

25 INT. GITTEL'S APARTMENT.

Later that morning.

GITTEL, MIRIAM's mother, stands at the entrance to the apartment, GITTEL is olive-skinned and has narrow, brown eyes of an undetermined shape, lined with half-moon circles and framed by straggly, grey eyebrows. She wears a wide pocketed, flowered housedress. Wisps of grey hair are visible from under her kerchief, tied behind her ears. Thin, earrings dangle from her extended ear lobes.

GITTEL stands with one hand on the doorframe, the other on the heavy steel door. The unlatched door chain swings back and forth.

The front door to the apartment has three locks. It opens up into a foyer which extends into a main room, or "living room".

The living room is decorated in a melange of white, gold and green monochromes. The carpet is forest green, the walls white and the upholstery, turquoise. An oversized pineapple shaped lamp with a diamond-like patterned

25 CONTINUED:

surface sits on a seashell scalloped table top. A grey and pink watercolor triptych of stylized ballet dancers hangs above a mahogany piano. The paino lid is closed. The sofa and two chairs are covered in stiff plastic covers.

ENTER MIRIAM.

MIRIAM brushes past GITTEL's outstretched arm. She eyes the fading, blue-green tattoo etched on the underside of GITTEL's forearm.

> GITTEL
> Where were you?

> MIRIAM
> I spent the night at my friend's place. Didn't she call you?

> GITTEL
> Your friend? What do I need to hear from your friend? Why didn't you call me?

> MIRIAM
> I didn't have the time.

> GITTEL
> You had time to call her but you didn't have time to call me?

> MIRIAM
> I'm sorry if you worried.

> GITTEL
> If I worried? What do you care? If you cared, you would have called. It's not nice a single girl running all over the city by herself.

> MIRIAM
> Ma. Don't worry. I'm not a child.

GITTEL turns and walks into the kitchen. She walks past white storage cabinets, a stove, refrigerator and sink. With effort, she sits in a plastic covered, upholstered high back chair at an oval, vinyl covered table.

> GITTEL
> (Firmly) Come over here.

                    MIRIAM
          What is it?

                    GITTEL
          What kind of question is that? I'm
          your mother.

                    MIRIAM
          Mom.

MIRIAM enters the kitchen.

                    GITTEL
          Where did you get those pants?

                    MIRIAM
          BLYTHE, my friend, lent them to me.

                    GITTEL
          You shouldn't wear them in this
          neighborhood. It's too religious.

                    MIRIAM
          No one saw me.

                    GITTEL
          That's what you think.

                    MIRIAM
          Ma. (Softly) Can I get you something?

                    GITTEL
          Like what?

                    MIRIAM
          A cup of coffee.

                    GITTEL
          I already had my coffee.

MIRIAM sits down on another chair. The seat cushion
squeaks.

                    MIRIAM
          GITTELEH, what are you going to worry
          about when I go to law school?

                    GITTEL
          What are you going to do with
          yourself?

                    MIRIAM
          What do you mean?

GITTEL
This running around. Zeh past nist.

MIRIAM
Whom doesn't it suit? And I'm not running around. I have a job. I have friends. What do you want me to do?

GITTEL shrugs her shoulders.

MIRIAM (cont'd)
I'm not going to wear long sleeves and sit in schul every day.

GITTEL
Who asked you to?

MIRIAM
I'm not part of that world. If I was, I should have been married at fourteen.

GITTEL
Nobody gets married at fourteen anymore. Eighteen, nineteen. They get to know each other first.

MIRIAM
How did we get into this conversation?

GITTEL
You said I want you to get married at fourteen.

MIRIAM
I didn't say that.

GITTEL
Anyway, what's wrong with getting married? You know how they say, "Alone is a stone".

MIRIAM
No, I don't. How would I know? I wasn't born in Europe. I was born in Brooklyn.

GITTEL
But it's still true.

MIRIAM
Mom, what are you saying?

                    GITTEL
          Mrs. Goldfarb called me. She wants you
          to meet her nephew, the medical
          student. He's tall and good-looking.

                    MIRIAM
          Oh.

MIRIAM rises and walks over to the refrigerator. She
opens the door. Dozens of small bowls, covered with
cellophane wrap crowd the shelves.

                    MIRIAM (cont'd)
          Any orange juice?

                    GITTEL
          What do you need orange juice?

                    MIRIAM
          I'm thirsty.

                    GITTEL
          You have to make it. There's a can in
          the freezer. Don't make a mess.

MIRIAM sighs as she opens the freezer door and withdraws
a cardboard can of orange juice. She shuts the door and
turns and withdraws a plastic pitcher from one of the
storage cabinets. She struggles with the metal lid of the
frozen juice container until it pops off. With a long
wooden spoon, she scoops the solid juice into the
pitcher. She fills the empty container with tap water and
pours it into the pitcher, mixing it with the spoon.

                    MIRIAM
          Want some?

                    GITTEL
          My sugar.

MIRIAM pours some of the juice into a glass and slowly
drinks.

                    MIRIAM
          I don't think I want to meet this
          person right now.

                    GITTEL
          Why not?

                    MIRIAM
          I'm not interested.

GITTEL
What are you interested in? A goy?
This is a nice Jewish boy who's
studying for a doctor. I know his
family. What's wrong with that?

MIRIAM
Nothing. It's just not for me.

GITTEL
You know, MIRIAM, I never figured you
for an idiot. Until now. You were
valedictorian, smaldictorian. You got
scholarships, certificates, awards,
but when it comes to common sense it's
an ausgeblausin ei.

MIRIAM
A what?

GITTEL
An empty egg.

MIRIAM
Thanks, Ma. I appreciate your support.

GITTEL
I didn't support you? Everything you
wanted to do, you did. Now, I just ask
one thing. Meet this medical doctor
almost and see for yourself. Don't
take my opinion. But to close your
mind. No. That's not smart.

MIRIAM
All right. I'll see him. Tell Mrs.
Goldstein or whatever her name is that
I'll go out with the big catch. She
can be the matchmaker.

GITTEL
Wait a minute. Don't do me any favors.
This is a lovely young man we're
talking about. He's not exactly a
meeskite.

MIRIAM
I'm sure he's a regular Clark Gable.
I'm going to change and then I'm going
out.

MIRIAM turns to exit the kitchen.

25   CONTINUED: (6)

>   GITTEL
>   (Voice rising) Go where?
>
>   MIRIAM
>   It's Fourth of July, Mom. I know that
>   they didn't have it in the old country
>   but here we shoot off fireworks. I'm
>   going to watch the fireworks with my
>   friends. Is that all right?
>
>   GITTEL
>   Fireworks. What does she need
>   fireworks?
>
>   MIRIAM
>   Yes, I know. (Rushing out) It's not
>   Jewish.

EXIT MIRIAM.

>   GITTEL
>   (Mumbling) I had enough fireworks in
>   my life.

FADE OUT:

26   EXT. DAY. BROOKLYN/QUEENS EXPRESSWAY. BROOKLYN, NY.

Later that day.

Lines of slow moving cars are headed toward Manhattan. The Manhattan skyline is visible ahead.

27   INT. MIRIAM'S CAR. CONTINUOUS.

MIRIAM glances at her wristwatch impatiently. She searches the radio dial but is unable to find any music that she likes. Raucous automobile advertisements blare through the speakers.

>   MALE VOICE
>   Stayed tuned for "Washington Round-
>   Up!"

MIRIAM shuts off the radio.

Flashback. 1957.

28   INT. DAY. BROOKLYN, NY. ELEMENTARY SCHOOL. REGISTRAR'S OFFICE.

MIRIAM is five years old. She is wearing a starched and ironed dress. Her hair is pulled back in a tight

28 CONTINUED:

ponytail. She stands at the desk of the REGISTRAR. She is accompanied by ABBA, her father. He is fifty years old. He wears a broad shouldered jacket, broad pants and carries a hat. His graying hair is combed back straight from the crown. The triangular folds of a handkerchief with the embroidered initials "AE" is visible in his jacket pocket.

> ABBA
> Good day, Madame. My name is Abraham Eisen. This my daughter, MIRIAM.

MIRIAM looks at the REGISTRAR suspiciously. The woman wears black framed glasses. A yellow pencil sticks out over her ear.

> REGISTRAR
> I had a note that she was registered at the Jewish girls day school.

> ABBA
> We changed our minds. I want MIRIAM to have an American education.

> REGISTRAR
> Do you have your papers filled out?

> ABBA
> Of course. (Hands forms to REGISTRAR)

> REGISTRAR
> (Examining forms) They look in order. (Takes pencil from behind her ear and corrects a word) We spell Kindergarten with a "t" not a "d".

ABBA winces.

> REGISTRAR (cont'd)
> School starts Monday at 8:45. Have her at the girls' entrance by 8:30. That's on the south side of the building. Her's a list of her necessary school supplies. She'll be having Miss Morgan. Any questions?

> ABBA
> No. Thank you very much.

> REGISTRAR
> How about you? (Looks at forms) MIRIAM? Any questions?

28   CONTINUED: (2)

ABBA and the REGISTRAR stare at MIRIAM. Something is troubling her. Finally, she speaks.

                   MIRIAM
    Do they--do they beat you in this
    school?

ABBA and the REGISTRAR stare at MIRIAM. Finally, the REGISTRAR laughs.

                  REGISTRAR
    Where did you get that idea?

                   MIRIAM
    I heard ABBA say that in Poland the
    teacher hit him on the hand with a
    ruler and it got swollened.

                  REGISTRAR
    Well, we don't beat the children.

MIRIAM appears uncertain as to whether or not to believe the REGISTRAR. ABBA shakes his head.

                    ABBA
    Let's go, MIRIAM. She will be to
    school on Monday morning.

ABBA turns to walk out. MIRIAM follows him dutifully. The REGISTRAR shakes her head and puts MIRIAM's forms on a pile of other forms.

                                      FADE OUT:

Flashback. 1960.

29   INT. DAY. LUNCHROOM. ELEMENTARY SCHOOL, BROOKLYN, NY.   29

MIRIAM's second grade class. The class is equally divided between Catholics and Jews. There is one Protestant girl in the class, INGER, a slender, blond. She stands apart. The others students open their cowboy and movie star lunchboxes and withdraw large sandwiches and tightly fastened thermoses containing soup or chocolate milk. They unwrap sandwiches containing thick slices of salami or sausage covered with mustard and pickles or piles of egg salad or tuna fish. INGER nibbles on a slice of cheese resting between two unseasoned slices of brown bread.

MIRIAM finishes her sandwich. She looks over at ALFRED. ALFRED is a chubby, black-haired boy in a horizontally striped tee-shirt. He is studying his Religious

Instruction book. It has colored drawings of saints and angels. She slides over to ALFRED.

MIRIAM
Can I see, ALFRED?

ALFRED grudgingly lets MIRIAM see the book.

MIRIAM (cont'd)
(Examing the pages) How do they know what angels look like?

ALFRED
(Growling) It's in the book.

MIRIAM
How do they keep their robes clean?

ALFRED
I don't know.

MIRIAM
Are you going to be a priest like Pasquale?

ALFRED
(Grabbing the book and moving away from MIRIAM) Are you crazy? He's got the calling.

MIRIAM
The what?

ALFRED
The calling.

MIRIAM
Who called him?

ALFRED
God.

MIRIAM looks skeptical. She glances down the bench at Pasquale, a soft, round-faced boy. He smiles at her.

MIRIAM
(Whispering) What does it mean to be a priest?

ALFRED
Don't you know anything? He can't get married.

                    MIRIAM
          He can still have friends, can't he?

                    ALFRED
          Yes. Why are you so interested?

                    MIRIAM
          Nothing. I just didn't know anything
          about it. I like that picture of the
          angel.

MIRIAM looks over at INGER. MIRIAM walks over to her.

                    MIRIAM (cont'd)
          Hi. How come you don't go to Religious
          Instruction with ALFRED and Pasquale
          and Cecila and the rest of the other
          kids?

                    INGER
          (Cooly) I'm Protestant.

                    MIRIAM
          Oh. What's the difference?

                    INGER
          We're not the same.

                    MIRIAM
          You're different?

                    INGER
          Yes.

                    MIRIAM
          I don't understand.

                    INGER
          We believe in different things.

                    MIRIAM
          Did the Protestant people and the
          Catholics have a fight or something?

                    INGER
          No.

                    MIRIAM
          (Smiling) Then why can't you make up?

Suddenly, a bell rings. The children, carrying their
lunchboxes line up, boys on one side of the lunchrooom,
girls on the other. INGER, empty-handed, walks alone. Led

29 CONTINUED: (3)

by their teachers, the children march out of the
lunchroom and down the hall. They pass the school
library. MIRIAM cranes her neck to peer inside. It is
empty and quiet and filled with light streaming from the
tall windows. Pink Japanese cherry tree blossoms are
visible through the windows. The librarian is seated at
the front desk. She sees MIRIAM and waves. MIRIAM smiles.

FADE OUT:

END FLASHBACK.

FLASH FORWARD TO SCENE 26.

30 EXT. DAY. BROOKLYN/QUEENS EXPRESSWAY. BROOKLYN, NY.

The cars are lined up bumper to bumper.

31 INT. MIRIAM'S CAR. CONTINUOUS.

A car horn blasts MIRIAM out of her reverie. She has
barely moved her vehicle. Wavy fumes of gasoline exhaust
distort the view. MIRIAM stretches her neck. An
overheated car has stalled in lane next to her, forcing
lanes to merge. Slowly, she passes the disabled vehicle.
Children in the back seat look at MIRIAM anxiously as the
adults argue in the front seat. In a moment, the traffic
lessens and MIRIAM enters the Brooklyn Battery Tunnel.
Her eyes blink rapidly, as they adjust to the darkness.

MIRIAM
(Whispering) I hope he waited.

FADE OUT:

32 EXT. SUNSET. CITY ISLAND, NY.

Later that day.

MIRIAM and RANDALL stroll the streets of City Island. It
is an island community resembling a New England
village.One and two story commercial buildings and
residences line the main street.

MIRIAM and RANDALL walk onto a pier. The pier houses a
seafood restaurant. Diners and wait staff are visible
through the plate glass. At the end of the pier, anglers
cast their lines and wait.

The sky darkens. One or two stars appear.

MIRIAM leans over the pier railing. RANDALL comes up
behind her and places his arm around her shoulders.

MIRIAM
I can't believe I lived in New York all my life and I never knew this place existed. (Breathing deeply) People actually live this close to nature and just a few miles there are all these abandoned apartment houses with broken windows and graffiti.

RANDALL
Someone in the Astrophysics Department told me about it. His brother is an intern at Montefiore Hospital in the Bronx and lives here.

MIRIAM
Have you ever been here before?

RANDALL
(Pausing) Yes.

MIRIAM
I meant if you had ever eaten in the restaurant before. The fish was so fresh.

RANDALL
They probably brought it in from New England. The waters here are polluted.

MIRIAM
I'm sure.

RANDALL
Have you ever been fishing?

MIRIAM
No. The only fishing I ever did was when I pointed to a live carp in the tank at the fish store and picked it out for my mother to make gefilte fish. I bought it home and it lived in the bathtub till she--ugh, clubbed it to death and ground it up in this metallic grinder she attached to a chair with a vise.

RANDALL
That's quite a story. I like listening to you.

MIRIAM
(Smiling) I like talking to you.

32 CONTINUED: (2)

> RANDALL
> We'll come here again if you like it.

> MIRIAM
> That would be great.

MIRIAM turns to look at the sky. Together they watch the exploding fireworks as the black water rushes beneath them under the pier.

FADE OUT:

33 INT. DAY. OFFICE. ASTROPHYSICS DEPARTMENT.

Next day.

MIRIAM sits at her typewriter, typing, overcome by her thoughts.

ENTER BLYTHE and DELORIS.

BLYTHE and DELORIS rush in and surround MIRIAM's desk.

> BLYTHE
> Share! Share!

> MIRIAM
> (Looking up) Share what?

> BLYTHE
> Coy aren't we? This can only mean one thing. You got DOWN the other night.

> MIRIAM
> Don't be ridiculous. I don't even know him.

> DELORIS
> He looks like a movie star. That actor in the movie about World War Two. Ooh- what's it called? Carol Baker was in it. She married him in the movie.

> MIRIAM
> James Shigata?

> DELORIS
> That's it.

> MIRIAM
> (Withdrawing a sheet of paper from her typewriter) No, he doesn't. That guy was Japanese.

BLYTHE
So?

MIRIAM
There's a big difference between Japanese and Chinese people.

BLYTHE
There is?

DELORIS
BLYTHE! That is so racist! They don't look alike at all. Japanese people are taller and their eyes go up, not down. Or is it the other way around?

MIRIAM
(Laughing) You're crazy, both of you. C'mon, let's get to work.

BLYTHE
(Stubbornly) I have an investment in this relationship. I got you into those sexy white jeans and I made get the ditch-the-mom 'phone call, so I want to know.

MIRIAM
(Hesitating) There's nothing to say. We saw the play. I drove him back to his apartment. Nothing happened. I changed my mind. I didn't go in or, you know, stay there. I went back to Brooklyn. That's all.

BLYTHE and DELORIS exchange glances.

DELORIS
Well, if it had been me that was alone with him, we would have gone round he world. He's fine.

MIRIAM
Thanks, girls. I appreciate your help. The play was great. You should see it. It ends Friday.

BLYTHE
Are you going to see him again?

MIRIAM
If he asks. Who's this John Dean who's testifying this morning? Turn it up,
(MORE)

33 CONTINUED: (2)   33

                    MIRIAM (cont'd)
               DELORIS. I don't want to miss
               anything.

MIRIAM puts a new sheet of paper in her typewriter.

                    DELORIS
               Have you see him on television? He has
               these funky little glasses. What a
               sleaze. Are you sure you want to be a
               lawyer, MIRIAM?

                    MIRIAM
               Ssh. I can't hear anything.

BLYTHE shrugs and turns up the radio volume.

                                                FADE OUT:

34   EXT. DAY. COLUMBIA UNIVERSITY.   34

Next week.

MIRIAM and RANDALL sit on a bench facing the quadrangle.
They are eating lunch.

                    MIRIAM
               Did you know that at the time they
               used to call Columbia, King's College,
               they used to graze sheep here?

                    RANDALL
               No. What else do you know?

                    MIRIAM
               I have no idea where I get this stuff.

RANDALL's thigh brushes against MIRIAM's. She starts.

                    RANDALL
               Is six o'clock okay? I'll pick you up
               at the office.

                    MIRIAM
               Yes.

                    RANDALL
               You seem quiet. Is everything all
               right?

MIRIAM lowers her eyelids.

                    MIRIAM
               In a few weeks, I'll be leaving. I
               have to start law school in Boston and
                         (MORE)

34 CONTINUED:

                    MIRIAM (cont'd)
               you'll be continuing your fellowship
               here at Columbia, so I guess we'll be
               saying goodbye.

                    RANDALL
               I don't think so. (Looking up) I'm
               going with you. I'm going to transfer
               to Harvard.

                    MIRIAM
               You mean live together?

                    RANDALL
               No. (Standing) Get married.

MIRIAM is mute, wide-eyed. She rises. RANDALL rises. They
embrace and kiss, oblivious to the smiling passers-by.

                                             FADE OUT:

35 INT. DAY. GITTEL'S APARTMENT.   35

Next week.

View of the vacant foyer and living room.

The sound of a doorbell is heard.

ENTER MIRIAM.

She opens the peephole and peers out. A very tall, young
man is standing there. She looks at his chest and
continues to look until she sees the top of his head. She
is compelled to bend her knees to view his entire frame.

                    BURTON
               Hi. I'm Mrs. Goldfarb's nephew. BURTON
               WEINER.

MIRIAM clangs the circular lid of the peephole shut. She
unlatches the door and opens it.

                    MIRIAM
               (Unlatching the door chain) Come in.

ENTER BURTON.

His head seems to touch the top of the doorframe. He
wears a madras plaid, short-sleeved shirt and khaki
colored pants.

                    MIRIAM (cont'd)
               She didn't say that you were so big.

                    BURTON
          Everyone says that.

                    MIRIAM
          Come in. (Leading the way into the
          living room) Have a seat.

BURTON sits on the sofa, beneath the window air-condi-
tioner. He rests his ankle on his knee and grasps it with
his large hand.

                    MIRIAM (cont'd)
          Can I get you something?

                    BURTON
          What do you have?

                    MIRIAM
          Seltzer and syrup.

                    BURTON
          No Coke?

                    MIRIAM
          Sorry.

                    BURTON
          That's all right. So you're going to
          law school?

                    MIRIAM
          Yes. In Boston.

                    BURTON
          Do you want to be a lawyer?

                    MIRIAM
          (Sitting down, it appears as if she
          might return a sardonic answer but she
          represses herself) Yes.

                    BURTON
          A lady lawyer. That's cool.

                    MIRIAM
          You're in medical school?

                    BURTON
          NYU. Third year.

                    MIRIAM
          A gentleman doctor. That's unusual.
          What are you interested in?

>   BURTON
>   In medical school?
>
>   MIRIAM
>   Yes.
>
>   BURTON
>   Surgery.
>
>   MIRIAM
>   I think I'll have a drink.
>
>   BURTON
>   Scotch?
>
>   MIRIAM
>   No, seltzer. We don't have any liquor.
>
>   BURTON
>   My grandmother used to drink that
>   stuff. This old man used to haul
>   wooden crates of it up the stairs to
>   her apartment in Williamsburg. 'Til
>   she died.

MIRIAM rises.

EXIT MIRIAM.

ENTER MIRIAM.

Kitchen.

MIRIAM is agitated. She withdraws a blue glass bottle of carbonated seltzer from the refrigerator. The air pressure in the bottle makes a hissing sound as she shoots the liquid into a glass. She replaces the bottle in the refrigerator. She sips the seltzer and places it on the counter. She turns to leave. She returns and places it in the sink, turning to leave again. She returns and picks the glass up, rinses it, then wipes it, then places it in the cabinet.

EXIT MIRIAM.

ENTER MIRIAM.

>   MIRIAM
>   Do you play basketball?
>
>   BURTON
>   No, golf.

35 CONTINUED: (3)

>   MIRIAM
>   Look. I may have made a mistake.
>
>   BURTON
>   No, it's tonight.
>
>   MIRIAM
>   You're right. I meant something else.
>
>   BURTON
>   MIRIAM, it's just a date. If you want
>   to go out to catch a movie or some-
>   thing, fine. If not, that's all right,
>   too.
>
>   MIRIAM
>   Blind dates are so awkward.
>
>   BURTON
>   Tell me about it. I don't get to meet
>   too many Jewish girls in the hospital.
>   As a matter of fact, I'm dating a
>   nurse. She's Irish and my parents are
>   having a heart attack. I agreed to
>   this to get them off my back.
>
>   MIRIAM
>   You know, (Smiling) this might work
>   out. I can use all the friends I can
>   get. Let's go. Something's playing at
>   the Loew's that I want to see.

MIRIAM and BURTON rise and walk towards the front door.
MIRIAM picks up her purse slung on the back of a door
handle and withdraws her apartment keys.

EXIT MIRIAM and BURTON.

MIRIAM busies herself with locking the front door.

>   BURTON
>   Have you been following the Watergate
>   hearings?

                                        FADE OUT:

36 INT. DAY. OFFICE. ASTROPHYSICS DEPARTMENT.   36

Next week.

MIRIAM, BLYTHE and DELORIS are seated at their desks.

36 CONTINUED:

> BLYTHE
> (Typing) After President Kennedy died, I no longer had any interest in politics.
>
> DELORIS
> (Laughing) What were you at the time? Thirteen.
>
> BLYTHE
> (Retorting) I was involved. I even had a straw hat that said "Kennedy/Johnson". If I could have voted I would have voted. MIRIAM! Did you like President Kennedy?
>
> BERNIE
> Vu Den?

ENTER BERNIE.

BERNIE is a short young man with glasses and a crew cut. He stands at the doorway, holding a sheaf of papers.

> DELORIS
> BERNIE SCHLOSSBERG! Back from D.C. so soon?
>
> BERNIE
> You wouldn't believe it. You can't even get around there. It's a media invasion. The whole world is watching. Did you girls miss me?
>
> DELORIS
> No!
>
> BERNIE
> Oh, yes you did. Who brought you your tunas on rye, pickles on the side and diet raspberry Dr. Brown, Cel-ray for MIRIAM? (Placing his papers on MIRIAM's desk) There aren't too many changes from NASA. I know that you think that your work is boring but it's going to get us into the satellite business. It's the wave of the future.
>
> MIRIAM
> Thanks, BERNIE. Did you go to the hearings?

BERNIE
No, but every television was on wherever you went. I couldn't believe that Butterfield. Just the way he dropped that bomb about Nixon's tapes. Isn't anything private anymore? Next we'll be hearing that Pat had leather pajama parties in the Oval Office. And they were smoking some killer weed. Not that I'd know about such things.
(Looking up as if speaking to a hidden microphone)

MIRIAM, DELORIS and BLYTHE laugh.

BERNIE (cont'd)

It's like all the grown-ups have spilled the beans.

MIRIAM
I wonder how it's going to affect our foreign policy.

BERNIE
(Turning towards MIRIAM) Now that I think of it, I heard something about your foreign policy. Are you dating RANDALL CHANG from the eleventh floor?

BLYTHE and DELORIS swing their chairs around.

MIRIAM
BERNIE, you know I only have eyes for you.

BERNIE
Oh, you say that but you never go out with me.

MIRIAM
I don't believe in summer romances.

BERNIE
Is she flirting with me?

DELORIS
I don't think so.

BLYTHE
But you didn't answer the question.

36 CONTINUED: (3)

                MIRIAM
        How nice of you all (returning to her
        work) to be so interested in my
        personal life.

BLYTHE, DELORIS and BERNIE exchange glances. BERNIE nods his head knowingly. He turns to exit and begins whistling.

                DELORIS
        (To BERNIE's retreating back) What's
        that tune?

                BERNIE
        The theme from "Bridge Over the River
        Kwai".

EXIT BERNIE.

                DELORIS
        Wasn't that Korea?

                              FADE OUT:

37 INT. DAY. DOCTOR'S EXAMINING ROOM.

Next week.

GITTEL is seated on a chair next to the examining table. Glass-doored cabinets are suspended from the ceiling. A dark-hued print of a woman winnowing wheat hangs on the wall. The woman's face is not visible. GITTEL wears a quilted dress made out of a shiny material. It has a fleur-de-lis print on it. Her skin is gray-looking. She wears a wig of billowing artificial fiber. A watch and ring press into her thickened wrist and finger.

ENTER DR. SCHULTZ.

DR. SCHULTZ, a young doctor, wears gold, wire-rimmed glasses and a white, lab coat with his name embroidered above the chest pocket in italic letters. A folded stethoscope protrudes from his pocket.

                DR. SCHULTZ
        How are you today, MRS. EISEN?

                GITTEL
        I'm here to check my pressure, DR.
        SCHULTZ. It seems to me to be high.

                DOCTOR SCHULTZ
        How do you feel?

37 CONTINUED:

                    GITTEL
          The same.

                    DOCTOR SCHULTZ
          Headaches?

                    GITTEL
          Why shouldn't I have headaches?

                    DOCTOR SCHULTZ
          (Reading her chart) How's your
          daughter, the lawyer?

                    GITTEL
          She's not a lawyer yet.

                    DOCTOR SCHULTZ
          Please be seated.

GITTEL rises and seats herself on the examining table.
Her small feet, clad in expensive and fashionable leather
shoes, dangle from the table. She unfastens her sleeve
and pushes it up over her elbow revealing the tattooed
number on her forearm.

                    DOCTOR SCHULTZ (cont'd)
          (Placing the blood pressure cuff on
          her upper arm, inflating the bulb and
          putting the stethoscope in his ears) I
          always wanted to ask you, MRS. EISEN,
          if you don't mind. Why don't you get
          rid of that? (He points to her fore-
          arm)

                    GITTEL
          Why should I take it off? Let them
          remember.

                    DOCTOR SCHULTZ
          Your pressure is somewhat elevated.
          (Releasing and rolling up the blood
          pressure cuff) Are you taking your
          medication?

                    GITTEL
          I have a whole table full of pills.

                    DOCTOR SCHULTZ
          Are you able to manage?

GITTEL
Do I have a choice? (She rolls her sleeve down and buttons it at the wrist)

DOCTOR SCHULTZ
The war must have been a terrible experience.

GITTEL
(Laughing) You have time today, DOCTOR?

DOCTOR SCHULTZ
A few minutes.

GITTEL
What do want to know?

DOCTOR SCHULTZ
My father was a chaplain in the U.S. Army. He saw things. He was in Buchenwald. He was born in Germany and spoke the language.

GITTEL
(Pausing) Catholic?

DOCTOR SCHULTZ
(Smiling) No, he was Protestant.

GITTEL
The same thing.

DOCTOR SCHULTZ
Well, actually they're not.

GITTEL
To me they are. You're from German parents and the son of my greatest enemy. But you didn't do a thing to me. So I have nothing against you personally. You're my doctor, isn't that right?

DOCTOR SCHULTZ
Yes, of course, but there is a difference between Catholics and Poles, I mean Protestants.

GITTEL
The Polish Catholics were worse than the Germans. They finished what the
(MORE)

37 CONTINUED: (3)

                    GITTEL (cont'd)
               Germans started. (She places her hand
               on her chest)

                    DOCTOR SCHULTZ
               I'm sorry I mentioned it.

GITTEL struggles to get off the examining table.

                    GITTEL
               Do you want to give me a prescription?

                    DOCTOR SCHULTZ
               No, just increase your medication by
               half a tablet. Can you remember that?

                    GITTEL
               I remember alot. (Picking up her purse
               and starting to exit) I have nothing
               against you personal, DOCTOR SCHULTZ.
               It's not your fault. Everyone lives by
               his own, kuvet, what you say,
               achievments. In this world and in the
               world to come.

EXIT GITTEL.

The door closes behind her.

                                                  FADE OUT:

38 INT. DAY. GITTEL'S APARTMENT.   38

Next morning.

MIRIAM is standing at the dining room window looking out
into the street. She sees men hurrying to early morning
prayers, their velvet prayer bags clasped tightly under
their arms. She turns away and examines the room. The
wallpapered walls are decorated with meandering vines. A
grinning black and white cat clock is hangs on the wall.
Its curled tail swings as if it were a pendulum. Its
whiskers indicate the time to be 7:30. The sound of shoes
clacking on linoleum is heard.

ENTER GITTEL.

GITTEL is wearing a kerchief and a housedress.

                    MIRIAM
               Good morning, Ma. Can I get you
               anything?

GITTEL holds up her hand to silence MIRIAM. GITTEL's lips
move noiselessly as she mumbles her prayers. She sits at

38 CONTINUED:

the table and begins to examine a tray of pill bottles. She makes a motion as if to drink. MIRIAM rises and goes to the refrigerator, opening the door. Numerous foiled objects shine under the overhead light. She removes a pitcher of apple juice and pours some juice in a glass. MIRIAM places the glass on the table and with her other hand adjusts GITTEL's kerchief which has fallen back on her crown. GITTEL nods. She swallow a pill and sips the juice.

GITTEL
A grosse dank.

MIRIAM
(Sitting down) What did the doctor say?

GITTEL
Nothing. What can he say? I'm getting old.

MIRIAM
Maa! Sixty isn't old.

GITTEL
It is when you had my life. Your father, olev hashalom, was only seventy-two when he died. He always talked about seeing you walk to the chupa. He didn't merit it. May he rest in gan eiden.

MIRIAM
I always wanted to ask you. What were his children like before the war?

GITTEL
I only met them once. Two boys. One was eight year old, the other was six. They had black hair and blue eyes.

MIRIAM
What were their names?

GITTEL
Who can remember? Their mother was my cousin. They all went to the ovens.

MIRIAM
But Daddy was hidden, wasn't he?

GITTEL
Yes, a gentile farmer hid him for the whole war.

MIRIAM
I can't imagine how he spent those years. When he came out, his whole world was gone. It was like science fiction.

GITTEL
What?

MIRIAM
Like a fiction. Like a story.

GITTEL
It wasn't a story. It was real.

MIRIAM
Tell me about the children.

GITTEL
Fine children. I bought each of them a chocolate bar. I was only a visitor.

MIRIAM
Did Daddy ever talk about them?

GITTEL
No.

MIRIAM
Never?

GITTEL
If you asked, he talked. Why do you want to know?

MIRIAM
I don't know, Ma. I was just thinking. I never got to talk to Daddy about anything important.

GITTEL
You never wanted to know.

MIRIAM
(Sighing) That's not true. Now, it's too late. (Her eyes fill with tears)

GITTEL
What are you crying about? Are you sick?

MIRIAM
No, Ma.

                    GITTEL
          So, what cana you do? Alot lost their
          children, their parents, their
          husbands. The last time I saw my
          mother and father was on the railroad
          tracks at Auschwitz. "Kum mein
          tochter, let us say good-bye" he said.
          He knew what was going on. What did he
          deserve to die? He was a religious
          man. He took strangers home for
          Shabbos every week. If the war hadn't
          come, who knows what might have
          happened. People got married. They
          hardly knew each other. They said,
          Hitler was the matchmaker.

The wall clock ticked noisily,

                    MIRIAM
          Did you love Daddy?

                    GITTEL
          Who knew from love? We were alone. I
          could see he was from a good family.
          When I went to his aunt, the one that
          came back from Russia, in her barrack
          in the DP camp, she had a white
          tablecloth for Shabbos, challah. The
          snows were so high. Your father bought
          me a pair of shoes for an engagement
          present. He was already working.

                    MIRIAM
          Did you look for relatives? How did
          you look?

                    GITTEL
          (Sipping the juice) They had lists.
          They made announcements on the radio.

                    MIRIAM
          There was no one?

                    GITTEL
          Nobody.

                    MIRIAM
          I wonder why Daddy wanted to get
          married again.

                    GITTEL
          What are you talking about? It's a
          commandment from God. There is no
                         (MORE)

GITTEL (cont'd)
greater blessing than to have
children. I named you after my mother,
Miriam, olev hashalom.

GITTEL rises and walks to the kitchen sink and rinses her glass. She places it on the drainboard.

GITTEL (cont'd)
So?

MIRIAM
So what?

GITTEL
How was the boy?

MIRIAM
(Blushing) What boy?

GITTEL
What boy she asks? How many young men
come here to ask you for a date? You
scare them away with all your
diplomas. Always talking, talking.
Sometimes it pays to listen. The
doctor! What about the doctor?

MIRIAM
Oh, Mrs. Goldfarb's nephew.

GITTEL
Who else?

MIRIAM
He was here. He took me to the movies.
He was nice.

GITTEL
So what should he do? Bite? Are you
going to go out with him again?

MIRIAM
Maybe.

GITTEL
Maybe! You're making me crazy. You're
going to finish what the Germans
started. What's the matter with you?
Don't you know how to get a boy
interested in you?

MIRIAM
Calm down, Mom, your blood pressure.

GITTEL
Calm down, she says. You're the one giving me a heart attack. Enough already with this life you're leading. It's a waste of time. You're getting older. I got news for you, the bloom is off the rose, mein kindt.

MIRIAM's expression is filled with rage.

MIRIAM
(Sputtering) I have a boyfriend.

GITTEL suddenly stands still. Her features, previously contorted in resentment, relax. A smile plays on her lips. She returns to the table and sits down, plying the tablecloth with her gnarled fingers.

GITTEL
You do? (Slowly) Why didn't you say so? What's his name?

MIRIAM is suddenly fearful and hesitant, regretting her outburst.

GITTEL (cont'd)
Don't you know his name? A boyfriend without a name.

MIRIAM
(Blurting it out) Cohen. Randall Cohen.

GITTEL
Randall. What kind of name is that for a Jew?

MIRIAM
His parents are American.

GITTEL
What do you expect? So where does he live with his parents?

MIRIAM
He lives in the city. His parents live in Massa-Massachusetts.

GITTEL
So far? What does he do?

MIRIAM
A scientist. A Ph.D. A doctor of
astrophysics. He's studying.

GITTEL
What's that, estro-what you call it?

MIRIAM
Space.

GITTEL
You mean like rocket ships?

MIRIAM
Yes.

GITTEL
From this a person can make a living?

MIRIAM
He teaches at Columbia University.

GITTEL
A teacher? A Professor?

MIRIAM
(Anxiously) Yes, Mom.

GITTEL
When are you going to bring him to the
apartment? I'll make a nice dinner.

MIRIAM
Soon. Well, Mommy, I'd better be
going.

GITTEL
Where?

MIRIAM
I'm going to BLYTHE's house. We're
going shopping.

GITTEL
All the way into the city?

MIRIAM
I promised.

GITTEL
Go. Bring me back a container milk and
a rye bread, no seeds. They get caught
in my partial.

38 CONTINUED: (7)   38

                    MIRIAM
          'Bye, I'll call you.

MIRIAM walks rapidly towards the front door, then slows down. She turns to look at her mother at the kitchen table. MIRIAM raises her hand, smiles weakly, opens the door and closes it behind her.

                                        FADE OUT:

39 INT. NIGHT. RANDALL'S APARTMENT.   39

That night.

MIRIAM and RANDALL are in bed. She sits astride him, her muscular thighs encasing him, pressing into his body. They heave together in symmetry. Her face registers curiosity, passion, surrender. She bends down and breathing heavily, kisses him, her eyes open to his perfectly proportioned face. She inhales his scent. His hand caresses her breast. Her body trembles. They both gasp. She rolls over and lays next to him, her hand resting above her head. He plays with her fingers. She rises and crosses the room, her curls brushing her shoulders. His hand on his still heaving chest, he watches her.

                    MIRIAM
          (Examining several terra cotta figures
          of mitre-headed men and women engaged
          in erotic poses) Where did you get
          these?

                    RANDALL
          They're pre-Columbian. Mayan to be
          exact.

                    MIRIAM
          I don't remember seeing them before.

                    RANDALL
          They were a gift.

                    MIRIAM
          (Suddenly anxious) From whom?

                    RANDALL
          From a friend.

                    MIRIAM
          Who? (Voice rising) That girl you used
          to date before me?

RANDALL sits up, a sheet draped around his lower torso, his upper body illuminated by the sole light in the room.

> RANDALL
> MIRIAM, come back to bed.

> MIRIAM
> I can't believe that you would display these--these things when I'm here.
> (Beginning to sob)

RANDALL walks over to MIRIAM. He wraps the sheet around them both. He picks up one of the sculptures as if to drop it. MIRIAM's hand shoots out to restrain him.

> MIRIAM (cont'd)
> No, don't. It's art.

> RANDALL
> Are you sure?

> MIRIAM
> Yes. They're very interesting.
> (Replacing the figure) I was just surprised, that's all. It's hard to imagine the ancients doing that.

> RANDALL
> If they hadn't, we wouldn't be here.

> MIRIAM
> Maybe if yours hadn't. They say the Mayans came to Yucatan from Canada after having crossed the Bering Strait land bridge from China.

> RANDALL
> MIRIAM, I can assure you your ancestors did the same thing.

> MIRIAM
> (Smiling) I don't think so. They were too busy cooking and baking and studying the Torah ...

RANDALL wipes the tears from her cheek.

> MIRIAM (cont'd)
> ... to do this.

39 CONTINUED: (2)   39

MIRIAM lowers herself, rests on her knees and places her tongue and mouth on his lower abdomen. RANDALL envelopes her with the sheet and thrusts his head back.

                                                         FADE OUT:

40 INT. DAY. OFFICE. ASTROPHYSICS DEPARTMENT.   40

Next day. Late afternoon.

MIRIAM is alone in the office. She is sitting at her desk. She looks at her desk calendar. It reads "August 1, 1974". She places her head in her hands and covers her eyes. She rises and grabs her purse and a phonograph album. She bangs her knee on the open drawer.

EXIT MIRIAM.

41 INT. HALLWAY. CONTINUOUS.   41

ENTER MIRIAM.

She walks rapidly to the elevator, presses the call button and enters.

ENTER MIRIAM.

42 INT. ELEVATOR. CONTINUOUS.   42

MIRIAM pushes the ground floor button impatiently. She hits the elevator door.

EXIT MIRIAM.

43 EXT. OFFICE BUILDING. CONTINUOUS.   43

EXIT MIRIAM.

She walks rapidly, clutching the album to her chest. Suddenly, she hears the squeal of brakes and jumps back. A delivery truck driver shakes his fist at her. She continues to walk, crossing several streets and avenues. Finally, she stops before a narrow, brownstone building. She examines a slip of paper in her hand. She mounts the steep steps. She stops before the iron-grated front door and rings the bell.

                    REBBETZIN
          Yes? Who is it?

                    MIRIAM
          (Shouting into the intercom) I'm
          looking for Rabbi Lustbader, please.

43 CONTINUED:

                    REBBETZIN
          He's not here.

                    MIRIAM
          I didn't have an appointment. I was
          just wondering if I could speak with
          him.

There is a long silence.

                    REBBETZIN
          Come up. Push open the door when the
          bell rings.

44 INT. BROWNSTONE. CONTINUOUS.   44

ENTER MIRIAM.

MIRIAM opens the heavy front door to the brownstone. She
faces a long, dark stairwell. A woman appears at the
upper landing. It is the REBBETZIN. She wears a long
dress similar to ones in nineteenth century photographs.
A rolled wig rests on her head.

                    REBBETZIN (cont'd)
          Over here.

MIRIAM climbs the stairs, holding onto the worn, wooden
bannister. As she draws closer, she bites her lip.

                    REBBETZIN (cont'd)
          The Rabbi went away for a concert.
          Every week a concert. They don't let
          him live. But come in for a minute. I
          am the Rabbi's mother, REBBETZIN
          LUSTBADER. Come in.

MIRIAM follows the REBBETZIN into a heavily draped room.
Bookshelves bearing dozens of leather volumes lean
against the walls. She sits on a stiff velvet armchair,
the bristling fabric piercing her thin summer clothes.
MIRIAM looks at the phonograph album she had been
carrying. She looks up at the REBBETZIN.

                    REBBETZIN (cont'd)
          What can I do for you?

                    MIRIAM
          I am an admirer of Rabbi Lustbader

                    REBBETZIN
          What's your name?

MIRIAM
MIRIAM EISEN.

REBBETZIN
Are you a Jew?

MIRIAM
Oh, yes. My father was a Kohain.

REBBETZIN
And your mother?

MIRIAM
She was born in Poland.

REBBETZIN
Is she Jewish?

MIRIAM
She was in Auschwitz!

REBBETZIN
So were others.

MIRIAM
She was there because she was Jewish.

REBBETZIN
You don't look Jewish.

MIRIAM
Oh, I'm one hundred percent.

REBBETZIN
So for what reason did you want to see the Rabbi, my son?

MIRIAM
I heard so much about him. I have his record. (Shows the album cover to REBBETZIN) He's unlike anybody else, any other rabbi I ever heard of him. I mean, he's a folk singer. He even looks like one.

REBBETZIN
(Smiling) He always looked like that. Now everybody copies him. But, he in California. Is there something I can help you with?

MIRIAM
(Breathing deeply) I had a question.
What does the Torah exactly say about
marrying a non-Jew?

REBBETZIN
(Folding her hands and placing them in
her lap) When the matriarch, Sarah
looked to find a bride for her son,
Isaac, she sent the servant, Eliezer
away, to go back to Avraham's former
home. She said that her son, her only
son, would not marry among the non-God
fearing nations.

MIRIAM and the REBBETZIN sat silently.

MIRIAM
Is every word taken literally?

REBBETZIN
Yes. Some people see more in it than
others.

MIRIAM
I see.

REBBETZIN
How do you feel about this young man?

MIRIAM
(Looking up) He's different.

REBBETZIN
Why?

MIRIAM
There's something about him, something
peaceful. He's bright, of course, but
he seems to have this confidence. If
it's raining, he says it's sunny.

REBBETZIN
(Smiling) A regular weatherman.

MIRIAM laughs.

REBBETZIN (cont'd)
And what if you have children? How
would you feel about them being
brought up in another religion?

MIRIAM
I hadn't really considered it.

REBBETZIN
These are things that people should think of before marrying.

MIRIAM
What about freedom of choice?

REBBETZIN
Our history has shown that we do not have that luxury.

MIRIAM
REBBETZIN, with all due respect, why should I have to bear the miseries of all past generations?

REBBETZIN
(Sighing) It's true. Our recent history has been a tragedy. But you must also know that being Jewish is a privilege.

MIRIAM
I don't see it.

REBBETZIN
On Rosh Hashanah, we promise to perform teshuvah, tzadakkah and tefilla. Do you know what they are?

MIRIAM
Not really.

REBBETZIN
"Repentance, justice and prayer." Even in a modern world these are positive goals. We are privileged because we are conscious that we are human beings and have a covenant with God. Can you imagine? We are constantly reminded that we must do these things on a daily basis. (Unclasping her hands) I'm sure that you will do the right thing.

MIRIAM
For whom?

REBBETZIN
For yourself, of course.

MIRIAM
REBBETZIN, I--. (Rising) Thank you for your time.

REBBETZIN
You're welcome. Wait, I want to give you a gift. (Rising, her stiff dress rustling) The Rabbi's latest record. From me to you.

MIRIAM
That's very generous.

REBBETZIN
Zie mit licht.

MIRIAM
(Pauses) My mother used to say that to my father when he used to go to work. I used to think it meant "Go with light". I think it really means "Be with light." They really didn't say much to each other, but I remember that.

REBBETZIN
We carry the burdens of those that went before us.

MIRIAM is startled as if the REBBETZIN had read her mind.

REBBETZIN (cont'd)
Did you know that Miriam, Moshe's sister was a prophet?

MIRIAM shakes her head.

REBBETZIN (cont'd)
She was loved by the people and loved by God because she led the people in song and dance and worship of God. Women are more spiritual, you know.

MIRIAM
Probably.

REBBETZIN
So go. Be like your aunt.

MIRIAM
My aunt?

44 CONTINUED: (5)
44

REBBETZIN
Your father was a Kohain. Moshe's brother Aharon was the first Kohain. Miriam was their sister, therefore she was your aunt.

MIRIAM
REBBETZIN, do you really believe all this stuff?

REBBETZIN
Absolutely.

MIRIAM
I wish I could, too. I once thought I did.

REBBETZIN
You will. (Taking MIRIAM's hand in her hands and kissing the top of her hair) Hashem has a plan for you. But you must look up to see it, not down. I wish I had been as lucky as you.

MIRIAM
I don't understand.

REBBETZIN
You have been chosen for this challenge.

MIRIAM rises. Her arms filled, MIRIAM exits the room and descends the stairway. She opens the front door.

45 EXT. FRONT DOOR OF BROWNSTONE. CONTINUOUS.
45

MIRIAM descends the granite steps and hurries down the garbage strewn street.

FADE OUT:

46 INT. DAY. RANDALL'S APARTMENT.
46

Next week.

MIRIAM and RANDALL are sitting up in bed watching television.

MIRIAM
RANDALL, tell me something about your family.

> RANDALL
> What do you want to know?

> MIRIAM
> RANDALL, please turn off the television.

> RANDALL
> I'm watching the hearings.

> MIRIAM
> You can watch the summary on the evening news.

> RANDALL
> MIRIAM, you're getting bossy.

> MIRIAM
> Please.

> RANDALL
> (Sighing, he clicks the remote control) What?

> MIRIAM
> What are they like?

> RANDALL
> Let's see. Typical dysfunctional Chinese family.

> MIRIAM
> (Leaning on her elbow) I don't believe it.

> RANDALL
> Overachieving driven immigrants?

> MIRIAM
> How did they get out of Communist China?

> RANDALL
> I don't know the details. They kept me out of it. I think my father went first on some sort of conference and my mother and I were smuggled out later. It was kind of cloak and dagger. They left everyone behind.

> MIRIAM
> Why did they do it?

RANDALL
Disillusioned, I guess. They had been party-liners. They saw things they couldn't reconcile.

MIRIAM
Like what?

RANDALL
Prisons, Gulags. Despite the repression, people talked. At great risk. People disappeared, sometimes, for thinking.

MIRIAM
What about religion?

RANDALL
In China, religion was outlawed.

MIRIAM
How were they raised?

RANDALL
Buddhists. Now they're Methodists.

MIRIAM
And you?

RANDALL
A little bit of this, a little bit of that.

MIRIAM
What about you?

RANDALL
I'm me.

MIRIAM
How were you brought up?

RANDALL
Methodist. But I used to visit my friend, Simon's synagogue. He was Orthodox I can speak a few words of Yiddish.

MIRIAM
You never told me!

RANDALL
You never asked.

MIRIAM
Why can you say?

RANDALL
Auf dere gesught.

MIRIAM
(Collapsing in laughter) I can't believe it. Your accent is better than mine. This is so weird.

RANDALL
Why? Where is it written that a Chinese can't learn Yiddish?

MIRIAM
Stop! I can't take it!

RANDALL
Okay. Let's watch the hearings.
(Clicking on the remote)

MIRIAM
One thing. Can you speak Chinese?

RANDALL
I understand it. My parents wanted me to learn English.

MIRIAM
RANDALL, I love you. You're my tzatzkelah.

RANDALL
I don't know what that means.

MIRIAM
Something between a teddy bear and a kitten. I'm not sure.

RANDALL
Ssh. It's Senator Ervin.

MIRIAM
(Murmuring) Wouldn't it be great if you could speak Yiddish with my mother?

RANDALL
(Muting the television sound) Why can't I?

46 CONTINUED: (4)   46

                    MIRIAM
          (Anxiously) Well, someday.

                    RANDALL
          When?

                    MIRIAM
          Not now. Her health isn't very good.

                    RANDALL
          It's probably not bound to improve.

                    MIRIAM
          I'll work on it. I promise.

                    RANDALL
          If this is going to be a problem, let
          me know. Maybe you should be going out
          with a guy who you would be willing to
          introduce her to.

                    MIRIAM
          All right. I'll arrange it.

                    RANDALL
          (Leaning over to kiss her) Good.

                    MIRIAM
          (Rolling out of bed) Um, I need a
          glass of water. (Tugging at her shirt
          that had gotten trapped under his
          body) Excuse me.

     RANDALL raises the volume on the television set.

                                                    FADE OUT:

47   INT. NIGHT. GITTEL'S MOTHER'S APARTMENT.   47

     Later that night.

     ENTER MIRIAM.

                    MIRIAM
          (Opening the door) Ma!

                    GITTEL
          (Wild-eyed) I know you went to
          college, but this is my house. Do you
          know what time it is? One o'clock in
          the morning!

MIRIAM
All right. I'm sorry. I got busy.
(Locks the front door)

GITTEL
No, Missus, what you're carrying on is
terrible. I curse the day you ever
bought a car.

MIRIAM
(Places her keys on the kitchen
counter, then reconsiders and retrievs
them) I earned the money myself.

GITTEL
I'm sorry. This can't be.

MIRIAM
Ma. Please go to bed. It's late.

GITTEL
Don't tell me what time it is. I've
been waiting for you all night.

MIRIAM
I told you I was going to be late.

GITTEL
One o'clock in the morning?

MIRIAM
(Trembling, MIRIAM whirls around) I
can't live your life! Ma, please. I'm
trying my best to please everyone.
It's driving me crazy!

GITTEL
What are you talking about?

MIRIAM
Nothing. I'm tired.

GITTEL
That nephew of Mrs. Goldfarb called,
the medical student. I didn't know
what to tell him. Where could I say
you were?

MIRIAM
You don't have to say anything.

GITTEL
He sounds like a fine boy.

47   CONTINUED: (2)

> MIRIAM
> He's all right.
>
> GITTEL
> All right? All right, she says? I don't see them breaking down your door.
>
> MIRIAM
> Ma! Enough!

GITTEL slaps a piece of paper down on the kitchen counter. It flutters to the floor.

> GITTEL
> Here's his telephone number. I'm not your secretary.

Painfully, GITTEL walks out of the room.

EXIT GITTEL.

MIRIAM bends down and retrieves the note. She examines the handwriting. The cursive lines are labored and awkward. The numbers have loops. The "9" looks like an "8". She places her head against the glossy, white kitchen cabinet doors. Something prevents them from closing completely. She opens one of the doors and retrieves a blue and white tin container, a charity box. A blurred photograph of a group of orphans is printed on a side of the box. The orphans' teachers and rabbis stand in the rear of the photograph before a planked wooden fence. She shakes the box. It is empty. She stares intently at the photograph.

Replacing the box, she slams the cabinet doors shut.

FADE OUT:

48   INT. DAY. LIBRARY. COLUMBIA UNIVERSITY.   48

Next day.

MIRIAM is walking down the library aisles, past dark, stacks of books. She looks drawn and somber. She fingers the bindings of the books as she walks. Slowly, the sounds of wheeled carts, footsteps, exaggerated whispers, fade.

FLASHBACK. 1960.

49 INT. DAY. GITTEL'S APARTMENT.   49

   ABBA and GITTEL are arguing. Their words cannot be heard.
   ABBA's face grows more and more enraged. GITTEL looks
   spiteful and sarcastic. It is clear that her remarks have
   met their mark. Young MIRIAM, strangely formally dressed
   with a starched shirtwaist dress is sitting on an
   upholstered chair. Lace doilies cover the armrests. She
   looks back and forth between ABBA and GITTEL. The
   television is on. A cartoon program is being broadcast.
   An animated locomotive looks about to burst. MIRIAM looks
   at ABBA. His eyes bulge and spittle dribbles from his
   mouth. MIRIAM makes no obvious gesture but her dimpled
   hand grasps one of the doily and rolls it under her
   fingers.

   FLASH FORWARD. LATER THAT YEAR.

50 INT. DAY. BROOKLYN, N.Y. NEIGHBORHOOD LIBRARY.   50

   MIRIAM is standing at the library checkout counter. She
   puts about eight books on the counter. The books are
   volumes of fairy tales, i.e., "THE RED BOOK OF FAIRY
   TALES", "THE BLUE BOOK OF FAIRY TALES", etc., and
   biographies, i.e., Ghandi, Eleanor Roosevelt, etc. She
   hands the librarian her library card. The librarian runs
   the card under a light and returns the books to MIRIAM.
   MIRIAM places them into a wheeled, wire shopping cart and
   starts to pull the cart behind her.

   EXIT MIRIAM.

51 EXT. BROOKLYN, NY. NEIGHBORHOOD LIBRARY. CONTINUOUS.   51

   MIRIAM retrieves a book from the shopping cart and starts
   to read and walk. Passersby look at her, bemused. She is
   in a world of her own. She reaches the intersection and
   almost forgets to stop. She closes the book and presses
   it to her chest and crosses the street. As soon as she
   reaches the other side, she begins to read again.

   FLASH FORWARD. 1965.

52 EXT. DAY. PROSPECT PARK, BROOKLYN, NY.   52

   Dust rises as thousands of young people, dressed in
   holiday finery enter the park. They are Jews celebrating
   the holiday of "Tashlich" in which they pledge to "throw
   away" their sins represented by bread crumbs, into a
   running body of water. They are gay and animated. It is
   one of the few occasions that Orthodox young girls and
   boys can mix freely. MIRIAM is walking with two
   adolescent girls. She is wearing high heeled shoes and

52 CONTINUED:

her feet, unused to adult footwear, are paining her. Still, she is exhilarated. Other park visitors, picnickers, ballplayers and strollers look at the horde with amusement.

MIRIAM and her friends throw bread crumbs to the ducks who flee in confusion and fear. She reads from a prayer book that she shares with another young girl.

53 INT. NIGHT. GITTEL'S APARTMENT.

Later that night.

MIRIAM is seated at the kitchen table. GITTEL is on her knees bathing MIRIAM's feet in a pan of Epsom salts. ABBA, standing off to the side, laughs. GITTEL throws a hostile glance at ABBA. GITTEL looks up at MIRIAM with love, admiration and concern. MIRIAM is wild-eyed with spiritual ecstasy.

> ABBA
> So, did you learn anything?

> GITTEL
> Ssh!

> MIRIAM
> I couldn't believe it. All those people. I never saw so many kids. They all know each other from school. The girls do, but they were nice to me. One girl, I met, FAY has eight brothers and sisters.

> ABBA
> A few more and they'd have a minyun.

> GITTEL
> Enough!

> MIRIAM
> I'm going to go to FAY's schul on Shabbos. She's coming to the house. If that's all right with you.

> GITTEL
> You have to ask? See, if you are with the right people, you meet nice people.

> MIRIAM
> She is nice. She's very pretty, too. Her mother just had a baby.

53 CONTINUED:

>   ABBA
>   And she'll have another one next year.
>
>   GITTEL
>   So what's wrong? We have to make up
>   for the six million we lost. I wish I
>   had been able to have more.
>
>   ABBA
>   Ach!

EXIT ABBA.

MIRIAM bites her lip.

>   MIRIAM
>   Why didn't you have more children,
>   Mommy?
>
>   GITTEL
>   (Rising and wiping her hands on a
>   dishtowel) God didn't will it.
>
>   MIRIAM
>   I would have liked a brother or
>   sister. Especially a sister.
>
>   GITTEL
>   I tried. I went from doctor to doctor.
>
>   MIRIAM
>   Do you think I could get a new dress
>   for Shabbos? FAY wants to go to a
>   dance at the Young Israel after
>   Shabbos. She asked if she could change
>   her clothes here. I said okay.
>
>   GITTEL
>   A dance? Hasidic people don't go to
>   dances.
>
>   MIRIAM
>   They don't?
>
>   GITTEL
>   No. Did you say she was coming this
>   Shabbos?

Exit GITTEL.

MIRIAM picks up her feet and examines the sole of her left foot.

53 CONTINUED: (2)   53

                                                    FADE OUT:

54   INT. NIGHT. LARGE ROOM.   54

     Later that week. Saturday evening.

     MIRIAM dressed in a new lavender shirtwaist dress which
     she smooths and tugs. The room is filled with young boys
     and girls. The boys wear skullcaps, the girls dresses or
     shirts and skirts. Recorded music is being played. No one
     dances but the young people eye each other with interest.
     A long table is set up holding soda, punch and cookies.
     MIRIAM stands alone, somewhat fidgety. She begins to look
     around the room as if looking for someone. Finally, she
     exits the room.

     EXIT MIRIAM

     MIRIAM descends a flight of stairs.

                         MIRIAM
                    FAY? Are you there?

56   EXT. NIGHT. BUILDING.   56

     MIRIAM exits the building. She passes several boys and
     girls standing at the entrance to the building, talking
     and laughing. She walks to the darkened street and looks
     across, than in both directions. She turns and starts to
     walk back into the building, then changes her mind and
     walks towards a darkened alley adjacent to the building.
     She continues to walk, backlit by the street light. She
     hears muffled sounds.

                         FAY
                    (Whispering) Stop, you'll mess up my
                    hair.

     MIRIAM sees FAY pressed up against the brick wall of the
     building. A tall, young man is kissing her neck, his hand
     pressed against her breast. They kiss passionately, the
     young man insistent, FAY not unwilling. MIRIAM continues
     to watch, mesmerized. The young man begins to unbutton
     the front of FAY's blouse. Her white brassiere is visible
     in the faint light. MIRIAM starts to walk backwards,
     silently, slowly. Her expression is one of curiosity and
     fear. She reaches the front of the building. The young
     people are still there.

                         GIRL
                    Who are you looking for?

56 CONTINUED:

                    MIRIAM
               Never mind.

Suddenly, MIRIAM sees a handsome young man under the
streetlight. He is older than the teenagers.

                    GIRL
               That's Simmy Keller. He goes to
               Brooklyn College.

                    MIRIAM
               I don't know him.

SIMMY looks at MIRIAM. He smiles and passes her.

                    SIMMY
               Hi.

He ascends the steps to the building. MIRIAM stares at
him intently. He turns to look at her again and enters
the building. Suddenly, MIRIAM grows cold and embraces
herself. She starts to walk off into the dark.

END FLASHBACK.

57 INT. DAY. LIBRARY. COLUMBIA UNIVERSITY. CONTINUOUS TO   57
    SCENE 48.

A LIBRARIAN approaches MIRIAM as she stands near the
stacks.

                    LIBRARIAN
               Are you looking for something in
               particular?

                    MIRIAM
               (Looking up) Well, I forgot to look it
               up in the card catalogue when I came
               in. I'm looking for Chinese history.
               Do you know where it is?

                    LIBRARIAN
               That's pretty broad. Anything in
               particular?

                    MIRIAM
               Not really.

                    LIBRARIAN
               (Turning) Follow me.

57 CONTINUED:

MIRIAM follows the LIBRARIAN as she leads the way between the stacks, turning left, then right, then left again. Finally, she stops.

> LIBRARIAN (cont'd)
> Here is our collection. We have some things on reserve. If you can't find what you're looking for, try the reference desk on the first floor.

> MIRIAM
> Thank you very much.

EXIT LIBRARIAN.

MIRIAM examines the rows of books.

MIRIAM suddenly stops. She turns her head sideways and reads the title "History of the Jews in China" imprinted vertically on the spine of a book. She withdraws the slim, dark green leather bound volume. The waxy pages fall open as she examines the book.

> MIRIAM
> (Voice Over) For a period of nine hundred years commencing in 960 A.D., there existed a colony of Jews in the city of Kaifeng, 470 miles south of Peking. The Jews were originally from Persia and had followed the end of the Silk Road to what was then the largest city in China. By the nineteenth century, most of the colony's members had assimilated into the native Chinese population.

MIRIAM slaps the book shut. Her expression is one of repose and concentration. Gathering her book bag, she turns and hurries out of the library.

FADE OUT:

58 INT. DAY. OFFICE. ASTROPHYSICS DEPARTMENT.

Later that day.

MIRIAM, BLYTHE and DELORIS are seated at their desks.

> BLYTHE
> Are you getting excited?

> MIRIAM
> (Looking up) About what?

58 CONTINUED:

                    BLYTHE
          About what? About moving to Boston?

                    MIRIAM
          Not really.

                    BLYTHE
          You're a strange bird, MIRIAM.

                    DELORIS
          Ditto.

                    BLYTHE
          Don't you feel a little something,
          changing your life and all?

                    MIRIAM
          I'm not. Anyway, I don't know if I'm
          going to go to law school this year.
          Maybe I'll take a leave of absence for
          a year.

BLYTHE and DELORIS sit silently.

                    BLYTHE
          DELORIS, did you hear that? She's not
          even going to go, when all we've heard
          this summer was law school this and
          law school that.

                    MIRIAM
          (Protesting) Wait a minute, I never
          said that.

                    BLYTHE
          I heard it. Did you hear it, DELORIS?

                    DELORIS
          Sure did, at least until that RANDALL
          character started sniffing around. It
          seems to me that after that we started
          hearing less and less about law
          school.

                    MIRIAM
          It's not that. I just have to re-
          evaluate if I want to spend three
          years studying to be a lawyer.

                    BLYTHE
          (Interrupting) In Boston, when Randy
          is in New York.

> MIRIAM
> No, you're wrong. Women shouldn't let men define their boundaries.

> DELORIS
> That's the way it is and that's the way it's always going to be unless you're independently wealthy or have a hormone deficiency.

> MIRIAM
> I don't agree.

> BLYTHE
> So you're giving up being a lawyer?

> MIRIAM
> I didn't say that. Maybe I'll go. I'm just in the process of thinking about it.

> BLYTHE
> I'd say you better speed up your thinking. You have just about run out of time.

> MIRIAM
> (Whispering) I know.

> DELORIS
> Anyway, maybe MIRIAM's right. The lawyers in the Watergate hearings all look like crooks. They knew what was going on. They probably did worse than Nixon. Can you imagine? I'm defending Nixon. They just didn't get caught.

The telephone rings. DELORIS picks up the receiver.

> DELORIS (cont'd)
> It's for you. (Points the receiver at MIRIAM)

MIRIAM rises. Her short skirt is stuck to the back of her thighs. She straightens her skirt. She takes the receiver from DELORIS.

> MIRIAM
> (To DELORIS) Thank you. Hello, this is MIRIAM EISEN. Who's this? Who? Oh, hi. How are you? My mother said that you'd called. (Turning her back to BLYTHE and DELORIS, mouthing "Excuse Me") Um.
> (MORE)

MIRIAM (cont'd)
I don't know. That sounds interesting.
A little complicated. Really? Do you
think so? I'll let you know. I'll get
a pencil. Okay. Got it. Yes, that's
what I wrote. I'll call you no later
than tomorrow at eleven. Thanks. You
have alot of imagination. 'Bye.

MIRIAM replaces the receiver and walks back to her seat.

MIRIAM (cont'd)
It was a friend about going away this
weekend. To the Catskills.

BLYTHE
The Catskills?

MIRIAM
Yes.

BLYTHE
What do you think that RANDALL will
have to say about it?

MIRIAM
I'll ask him.

BLYTHE
You think he's going to like you going
away with another guy?

MIRIAM
Oh, he's invited, too. And the
friend's girlfriend.

BLYTHE
A regular potpourri.

MIRIAM
(Murmuring) You have no idea.

BLYTHE
What did you say?

MIRIAM
Nothing. Let's get to work. (Returning
to her desk) BERNIE wants these things
finished before lunch.

BLYTHE
BERNIE can eat my lunch.

DELORIS
(Drily) He looks as if he already has.

58   CONTINUED: (4)

MIRIAM, BLYTHE and DELORIS laugh.

                                        FADE OUT:

59   INT. DAY. BURTON'S AUTOMOBILE. WEST SIDE HIGHWAY. NEW   59
     YORK, NY.

Four days later.

MIRIAM and RANDALL sit in the rear seat of BURTON black Lincoln Continental passenger car. BURTON and EILEEN, his date, sit in the front seat. BURTON is driving.

The car is traveling north on the West Side Highway.

MIRIAM looks thoughtful. She watches EILEEN closely. EILEEN watches BURTON with admiration and contentment. She has large blue eyes framed by black, fluttering lashes. Her features are limpid-looking as well. She is soft, pliable and pretty. Her auburn hair falls to her shoulders. She twirls their wavy ends and places them in her rosy mouth. MIRIAM looks at EILEEN with amazement, as if she is unable to determine if she is mentally disabled or very smart.

                    BURTON
          It's great that you could join us. You
          and EILEEN can share a room. But we'll
          have adjoining rooms, get it?

                    MIRIAM
          We got it.

                    BURTON
          EILEEN's going to dental assistant
          school.

                    MIRIAM
          Is she? I thought she was a nurse.

                    BURTON
          No, she's going to work for her
          father, Dr. Scharf, the dentist. He
          has a practice in your neighborhood.
          Do you know him?

                    MIRIAM
          On 48th Street?

                    BURTON
          Yes, that's the one.

59   CONTINUED:

> MIRIAM
> My mother goes to him. I thought
> EILEEN was a nursing student.
>
> BURTON
> Ha, ha. (Laughing uncomfortably) Noo,
> where would you get that idea?
>
> MIRIAM
> I must have been mistaken. (Settling
> down in the opulent leather seat)

EILEEN has been watching the exchange between MIRIAM and BURTON anxiously. Suddenly, she relaxes.

> EILEEN
> I know I'm not a nursing student.

MIRIAM glances at RANDALL. His profile is framed against the car window through which the grey Hudson River is visible. She looks at the passing apartment buildings, graffiti disfigured overpasses, abandoned red-brick warehouses. "SCHWARTZ & SON" reads one fading sign. The Lincoln rises up and down as it travels over the uneven pot-holed roadway.

> MIRIAM
> Good suspension.
>
> BURTON
> Lincolns are the best.

MIRIAM closes her eyes.

FLASHBACK. SUMMER, 1958.

60   EXT. DAY. CATKILLS, NY. BUNGALOW COLONY.   60

Sunset.

Young MIRIAM is running. Her hair is short. A plastic barrette pins it at the crown. She is wearing shorts and an off-shoulder white top. She passes screaming children throwing balls at each other. Off in the distance, GITTEL, wearing summer clothes, talks to a neighbor. MIRIAM speeds to the entrance of the bungalow colony. She finds a large rock and sits down. Cars pass, their headlights turned on, their tires crunching the gravel road. Fireflies appear. It grows dark. MIRIAM becomes anxious, then despondent. Finally, the car she has been searching for appears. It is ABBA. He is sitting in the front passenger seat, next to another man.

60 CONTINUED:

                    MIRIAM
          ABBA! ABBA! It's me. Wait! Don't go!

The car stops a few feet ahead of her. MIRIAM runs to
catch up with it. The door opens and MIRIAM enters. The
car moves on.

FLASH FORWARD. SUMMER, 1958.

61   EXT. DAY. SWIMMING POOL, BUNGALOW COLONY.   61

MIRIAM is in the pool with GITTEL. The plastered sides of
the pool are flaking and the water is cloudy. GITTEL
holds on to MIRIAM's hand as if afraid to let her go.
MIRIAM swims towards her mother. They hesitate. MIRIAM
embraces GITTEL warmly but GITTEL' return embrace is
weak. MIRIAM pushes off.

                    MIRIAM
          Watch! I can swim!

                    GITTEL
          I don't want you to swim. You might
          drown!

                    MIRIAM
          Watch!

MIRIAM manages to get away from GITTEL's grip. With great
kicking effort and much water swallowed, she swims to the
deep end of the pool.

                    GITTEL
          Come back!

62   EXT. DAY. PLAYGROUND. BUNGALOW COLONY.   62

MIRIAM plays on the swings. She finds that the harder she
kicks her legs the higher she goes. Her toes point tot
the clouds.

63   EXT. DAY. WOODS, BUNGALOW COLONY.   63

MIRIAM wanders in the woods and collects blueberries in a
pail. She finds a butterfly on a bush and watches it.
Soon it takes off, flying higher and higher among in the
sun streaked trees.

64   INT. DAY. GITTEL'S BUNGALOW.   64

GITTEL bakes the blueberries into a large, rectangular
cake. MIRIAM watches.

64 CONTINUED:

FLASH FORWARD TO SCENE 59.

65 INT. DAY. BURTON'S AUTOMOBILE.

> RANDALL
> What are you thinking about? (Touches MIRIAM's hand)

> MIRIAM
> I was just wondering. Did your mother ever make a pie?

> RANDALL
> What kind of pie?

> MIRIAM
> Any kind.

> RANDALL
> Yes.

> MIRIAM
> What did it look like?

> RANDALL
> What do you mean?

> MIRIAM
> Describe it.

> RANDALL
> A regular pie. With crusts and slits on the top.

> MIRIAM
> Did she press her fingers into the dough to make a design around the edges?

> RANDALL
> I really don't know.

> MIRIAM
> I'm sure she did. (Sliding back into her seat)

> RANDALL
> Anything else?

> MIRIAM
> I'm going to learn how make a pie.

65 CONTINUED: 65

>   EILEEN
>   (To no one in particular) Why bother
>   if the bakery can make it better?
>
>   BURTON
>   She's right.

EILEEN smiles.

>   MIRIAM
>   Just in case the bakery is out.
>
>   EILEEN
>   Well, that can happen. But you can
>   freeze them. Can't you, BURTON?
>
>   BURTON
>   Yes, Leeney.
>
>   EILEEN
>   I thought so.

MIRIAM looks at them incredulously. She looks at RANDALL. He is gazing out of the window.

The vehicle is approaching the Catskills. A barren rockface foothill looms above them. A single family home is perched at the apex.

>   MIRIAM
>   How far are we from Wurtsboro?
>
>   BURTON
>   About twenty minutes. Why?
>
>   MIRIAM
>   My father always said that if you made
>   it to Wurtsboro, you'd make it all the
>   way to the mountains.
>
>   BURTON
>   That's before they built the Thruway
>   and they had to crawl all over the
>   back roads. All the cars used to
>   overheat.
>
>   MIRIAM
>   I was just wondering.

MIRIAM suddenly looks panic-stricken as if she realizes that the trip had been a bad idea and would end in disaster.

                         MIRIAM (cont'd)
                    Does anyone have any gum?

                         EILEEN
                    I have a lollipop my father gives to
                    the kids. (Handing MIRIAM a red, heart
                    shaped lollipop)

                         MIRIAM
                    (Grabbing it) Thanks.

RANDALL turns to look at MIRIAM. MIRIAM mindlessly sucks
the lollipop and stares straight ahead.

                                                   FADE OUT:

66   INT. NIGHT. CATSKILLS HOTEL NIGHTCLUB. CATSKILLS, NY.   66

That night.

MIRIAM, RANDALL, BURTON and EILEEN are seated at a square
table in a nightclub. It is filled with well-dressed
patrons, most of whom are middle aged. They are watching
a COMEDIAN. The COMEDIAN wears a tuxedo. He carries a
hand-held microphone and roams the stage. The audience is
enjoying his performance. BURTON slaps his thigh in
response to the jokes. EILEEN has her elbows on the table
and frames her face with her hands, smiling at BURTON and
the COMEDIAN.

                         COMEDIAN
                    Dumbkopf! (Slapping his head) I forgot
                    the fleishike knife.

MIRIAM glances over at RANDALL. He has tears in his eyes
from laughter. She looks over at a black haired middle-
aged man seated near RANDALL. He is laughing so hard his
eyes narrow. She glances back at RANDALL and back at the
man.

                         MIRIAM
                    RANDALL, (Whispering) Are you sure you
                    aren't Jewish?

                         RANDALL
                    Who knows?

                         MIRIAM
                    Where was your family from in China?

                         RANDALL
                    Ssh. Not now. I can't hear him.

MIRIAM
Please. I have to know.

RANDALL
Near Peking.

MIRIAM
How near?

RANDALL
What difference does it make? You don't know one city from another.

MIRIAM
Please!

RANDALL
Four hundred miles or so.

MIRIAM
North or south?

RANDALL
You have to be kidding!

MIRIAM
North or south?

RANDALL
South.

MIRIAM
Were they from Kaifeng?

RANDALL
Where?

MIRIAM
This city south of Peking.

RANDALL
Can we discuss this later?

MIRIAM
No.

RANDALL
My mother was from a small town a couple of hundred miles from Peking. I haven't got a clue whether it was north or south. She moved to Peking when she was young. My father was from Peking. Satisfied?

66   CONTINUED: (2)

      MIRIAM
   Yes. Randy. Whatever you say. Anything
   you say is--do they still say swell?

      RANDALL
   I like her. Being worshiped can grow
   on you.

      MIRIAM
   You've been hanging out with Miss
   Congeniality too long.

      RANDALL
   MIRIAM! Schweig!

MIRIAM looks at RANDALL confidently.

               FADE OUT:

67   INT. DAY. GITTEL'S APARTMENT.

Two days later.

GITTEL is waiting in the foyer, her hands folded expectantly. MIRIAM pulls her rolling suitcase into the apartment. It wheels become trapped in the carpet remnants covering the rug.

      MIRIAM
   Ma! Get rid of these things. You're
   going to kill yourself one of these
   days and I'm not going to visit you in
   the hospital.

      GITTEL
   My daughter, if I'm dead you won't
   have to visit me.

MIRIAM and GITTEL laugh.

      MIRIAM
   You can be very funny, sometimes. Ma,
   remember that time when Mrs.
   Moskowitz's husband bought a house in
   the suburbs and Mrs. Moskowitz didn't
   want to move. She said she didn't know
   anybody. Her daughter, Sara, said,
   "You'll buy a dog and you'll walk the
   dog and you'll meet people." You said
   "Yeah, Sara's friend, Leah got a dog
   and all she meets are other dogs."

GITTEL shows no reaction.

                    MIRIAM (cont'd)
          It was funny on several levels. You
          visualized Mrs. Moskowitz meeting no
          one but dogs and Leah happened to be
          kind of--unattractive.

GITTEL continues to show no reaction.

                    GITTEL
          So how did it go?

                    MIRIAM
          The weather was very nice.

                    GITTEL
          I'm not interested if it rained.

                    MIRIAM
          BURTON is a nice guy but he's not my
          boyfriend. In fact, he has a girl that
          he likes and I think it's serious.

MIRIAM walks into the kitchen and searches for a glass.
GITTEL follows her.

                    GITTEL
          Another girl? For what reason did he
          invite you to come along? A fifth
          wheel? A chaperon?

                    MIRIAM
          (Into the top of her glass as she
          drank some water) Well, my friend
          came, too.

                    GITTEL
          What friend? That shiksha, Blanche?

                    MIRIAM
          BLYTHE. No, not her. (Swallowing hard)
          My friend, RANDALL, the scientist.

GITTEL circles around MIRIAM and then sits at the kitchen
table, watching her continuously.

                    GITTEL
          Who is this Rendell?

                    MIRIAM
          RANDALL with an "a". I told you about
          him.

                    GITTEL
          Rendell, RANDALL, what difference does
          it make?

                    MIRIAM
          I think it's nice to call someone by
          their right name.

                    GITTEL
          Yes?

                    MIRIAM
          (Walking over to the kitchen table and
          picking up a small, crystal vase)
          What's this? Something new?

                    GITTEL
          The bank gave it out for opening a
          certificate of deposit.

                    MIRIAM
          You opened a new account? Ma, you have
          a houseful of stuff. You don't need
          anything more. You have two
          televisions, a new set of pots.

                    GITTEL
          Are you making an inventory? Sit down.

MIRIAM sits uneasily.

                    GITTEL (cont'd)
          I'm waiting.

                    MIRIAM
          What do you want to know?

                    GITTEL
          How long have you been seeing this
          boy?

                    MIRIAM
          I mentioned him before. His parents
          live in Massachusetts.

                    GITTEL
          (Sighing) Today, everything is
          different. On the other side, no one
          ran around without their parents'
          permission. The parents knew best.
          When I married your father, there was
          no one to ask. My parents were dead. I
          know that you're not going to be the
                         (MORE)

GITTEL (cont'd)
wife of a Hasid. I have your father to thank for that, olev hashalom. He was a good Jew. No one could say anything bad about the Jews in front of him. But--he wasn't so religious. After the war, he thought he had enough. He was a good man, but he thought too much.

MIRIAM sat quietly.

MIRIAM
How are you feeling?

GITTEL
My eyes are bothering me.

MIRIAM
How's your pressure?

GITTEL
High enough. So, when are you going to bring this Rendell to the house?

MIRIAM
Soon.

GITTEL
So, what's going to be, MIRIAM?

MIRIAM
What do you mean?

GITTEL
Are you planning to go to Boston or stay?

MIRIAM
I don't know.

GITTEL
I think maybe you'd better bring this fellow over as soon as possible. Maybe he's not worth it.

MIRIAM
(Quickly) He is.

GITTEL
I see. So, that's the way it is. Remember, my daughter, like my mother used to say "Ah kish und ah glet bleibt nist ken fleck". A kiss and a touch doesn't leave a mark.

MIRIAM
Thank you, mother, for that sex education lesson.

GITTEL
What are you talking about? (Pausing) Mrs. Adler from the fourth floor told me she could put her hand in the fire that her Marsha is a good girl. Can I say the same thing?

MIRIAM
I don't really want to discuss it.

GITTEL
I asked you a question.

MIRIAM
You tell Mrs. Adler (Fuming) that if I were her, I would keep some ice around.

GITTEL
What are you saying?

MIRIAM
Nothing.

GITTEL
MIRIAM, this is it. Sunday, at two o'clock. We'll have bagels and lox. If you don't bring him, I'll know something is not right. That's it.

MIRIAM
Ma. I have to check with him first.

GITTEL
You have a whole week. If he's not here, I'll know. I'm not a fool, you know.

MIRIAM
(Interrupting) Please don't tell me that one about someone spitting in your face telling you it's raining. I can't stand that expression.

GITTEL
Just so you understand.

67   CONTINUED: (5)

                    MIRIAM
          What happened with the Watergate
          hearings while I was away?

                    GITTEL
          Everybody wants to sue everybody else.
          I never saw anything like it. They
          have no respect for the President. The
          only people that are going to get
          something from this are the Communists
          and the Araba.

                    MIRIAM
          That's an interesting point of view.

                    GITTEL
          Take my advice. They're going to hurt
          the government and then the others
          take over.

                    MIRIAM
          I don't see any camels attacking the
          White House.

                    GITTEL
          (Rising) Laugh all you want. I lived
          through it. A weak country is a
          danger.

EXIT GITTEL.

MIRIAM puts her arms down on the vinyl tablecloth and lowers her head.

                                        FADE OUT:

68   INT. NIGHT. MIRIAM'S BEDROOM.

That night.

MIRIAM, in nightclothes, sits up in bed. There is one single, twin bed in the room. The room is filled with juvenile furniture. MIRIAM's diplomas hang neatly above her desk. Aside from the diplomas, there are no personal items visible in the room. MIRIAM leans on her elbow and reaches behind her to open one of the sliding doors located in the headboard. She retrieves a woven straw basket. She raises the lid and uncovers two dolls dressed in Chinese costumes. She runs her fingers over their delicate bisque faces.

FLASHBACK. 1959.

69   INT. DAY. NEW YORK COLISEUM. FLOWER SHOW. NEW YORK, NY.   69

Young MIRIAM is skipping along the flower packed aisles, her crinolined skirt bouncing with the motion. Purple, white, yellow, orange and pink blossoms crowd the floors. She is with ABBA. She looks up at him with pleasure.

          ABBA
(Pointing to two china dolls in a basket) Would you like this?

MIRIAM nodded with anticipation.

          ABBA (cont'd)
(Quietly) I could have gone to Shanghai before the war.

          MIRIAM
Oh, ABBA, they're beautiful. Are they married?

          ABBA
If you want them to be, MIRIAM.

          MIRIAM
This one's the daddy, the one with the hat and this one's the mommy. What shall I call them?

          ABBA
Yenta and Mordcha.

          MIRIAM
Daddy!

          ABBA
What would you like to call them?

          MIRIAM
The lady is O-lan from the library book, "The Good Earth" and the man is, his name is--

          ABBA
Charlie Chan?

          MIRIAM
Do you know any Chinese names, Daddy?

          ABBA
I told you, Charlie Chan.

69 CONTINUED:

              MIRIAM
     Was Charlie Chan Chinese?

              ABBA
     What else? You think he was Jewish?

              MIRIAM
     All right. Charlie. Thank you, ABBA,
     thank you. I love you.

FLASH FORWARD TO SCENE 68.

MIRIAM looks around the room. She replaces the dolls and turns off her night table lamp. She is illuminated by the street lighting. The roar of a bus fills the room. Tears form in her eyes.

                                      FADE OUT:

70 INT. DAY. RETAIL STORE. BROOKLYN, NY.

Later that week. Sunday morning.

MIRIAM stands before the bakery counter. She rests her hand on the handle of a wire shopping cart. Behind the counter, MR. FARBER is handing change to MIRIAM.

              FARBER
     That's it, MIRIAM? Delivery today?

              MIRIAM
     No, I'll take it with me.

              FARBER
     (Handing MIRIAM her purchases, packed
     in brown paper bags) When are you
     going away?

              MIRIAM
     Soon.

              FARBER
     We're all proud of you.

              MIRIAM
     Thank you. How's your brother?

              FARBER
     (Shrugging his shoulders) Not so good.

              MIRIAM
     I wish him a complete recovery, a
     refuah shalomah.

70 CONTINUED:

                    FARBER
          Oo-main. I'll tell him you asked for
          him.

                    MIRIAM
          'Bye.

                    FARBER
          Oy, what do you say? President Nixon,
          he resigned.

                    MIRIAM
          What?

                    FARBER
          I heard it on the radio.

                    MIRIAM
          I missed it!

                    FARBER
          They were going to what-do-you call
          it, impeach him, so he quit.

                    MIRIAM
          I knew that the House of Representa-
          tives was considering it but I didn't
          think it would go this far.

                    FARBER
          It's history!

                    MIRIAM
          I guess it is. Thank you, Mr. FARBER.
          I'll see you later.

EXIT MIRIAM.

71 EXT. DAY. GITTEL'S APARTMENT HOUSE, BROOKLYN, NY.   71
    CONTINUOUS.

    MIRIAM greets people whom she recognizes, stops to chat
    with them and walks on.

72 INT. DAY. GITTEL'S APARTMENT. CONTINUOUS.   72

    ENTER MIRIAM.

    The sound of running water is heard.

    MIRIAM wheels the shopping cart into the kitchen. She
    unpacks the cart. She opens a cabinet and removes a linen

72 CONTINUED:

table cloth. She flings it over the vinyl table cloth and smoothes it out. She removes white dishes from the cabinets and sets the table for three place settings. She arranges the silverware and table napkins. She displays the food, bagels, lox, cream cheese, cucumbers and tomatoes. She adjusts the temperature on the percolated coffee. Pulling the folded shopping cart, she enters the foyer and picks up the carpet remnants and places them in a closet together with the shopping cart. She returns to the kitchen. She sits down at the table and waits.

ENTER GITTEL.

     GITTEL
  (Indicating the table) Very nice. See,
  if you want to you can do it.

     MIRIAM
  Ma--

     GITTEL
  Zipper my dress.

MIRIAM rises and walks over to her mother. Her open zipper reveals a rounded cervical spine.

     MIRIAM
  Stand straight, Ma.

     GITTEL
  You wait until you get old.

MIRIAM fastens the zipper.

     MIRIAM
  Very pretty. See, if you want to, you
  can get out of a housedress.

     GITTEL
  What are you talking about? People
  tell me I'm the best dressed woman in
  schul.

     MIRIAM
  In schul, yes, but in the house,
  you're a schlump.

     GITTEL
  For what should I dress up? To clean?
  What time is this young man coming?

     MIRIAM
  Two o'clock.

                    GITTEL
          What time is it now?

                    MIRIAM
          One forty-five.

                    GITTEL
          Is he the type of person who is on
          time?

                    MIRIAM
          Yes, Mom.

                    GITTEL
          What did you say he father is?

                    MIRIAM
          His father is a professor and his
          mother is a medical doctor.

                    GITTEL
          What kind?

                    MIRIAM
          Cancer.

                    GITTEL
          Did I tell you Mrs. Weiss down the
          hall, she has cancer?

                    MIRIAM
          No!

                    GITTEL
          They took off a breast.

                    MIRIAM
          I didn't know.

                    GITTEL
          How should you to know? You're never
          home.

                    MIRIAM
          Ma--

                    GITTEL
          What?

                    MIRIAM
          You'll be nice to him, no matter what?

72   CONTINUED: (3)   72

                        GITTEL
              What kind of question is that? What am
              I going to do? Shoot him?

                        MIRIAM
              No, but--

                        GITTEL
              Don't worry. Worry about yourself. I
              know how to behave.

                        MIRIAM
              Thanks, Ma.

     MIRIAM and GITTEL wait in silence as the arms on the
     black cat's belly move.

                                                     FADE OUT:

73   INT. DAY. GITTEL'S APARTMENT. CONTINUOUS.   73

     MIRIAM opens the door.

     RANDALL stands in the hallway, holding flowers wrapped in
     green tissue paper and a ribboned bottle of wine. He
     wears a light colored jacket and a white shirt and blue
     pants. A silk tie with diagonal stripes hangs loosely
     from his neck.

                        RANDALL
              (Holding up the wine) It's kosher.

                        MIRIAM
              Come in.

     RANDALL enters the brightly lit room. GITTEL approaches
     RANDALL, hesitates, then offers her hand. RANDALL rushes
     up to her.

                        RANDALL
              You must be MIRIAM's mother. You look
              just like her.

                        GITTEL
              Who else should she look like?

     GITTEL and RANDALL examine each other.

                        GITTEL (cont'd)
              Come in, sit. (Leading the way) This
              is our living room.

MIRIAM
(Hesitating) RANDALL, this way.

MIRIAM, GITTEL and RANDALL sit on the sofa.

RANDALL
(Indicating the highly polished mahogany piano) Do you play, MIRIAM?

MIRIAM
I used to.

GITTEL
Thousands of dollars and she can play one song.

MIRIAM
Ma!

GITTEL
Tell me, young man, where do you live?

RANDALL
Manhattan.

GITTEL
Were you born there?

RANDALL
No.

MIRIAM
(Rising) I think we should eat. I can't stay all afternoon. We have plans.

RANDALL
We do?

MIRIAM
Yes. You forgot. We're going to join BLYTHE and DELORIS to see that Italian film at the Odeon.

RANDALL
Oh, that's right.

The window air conditioner rattles noisily. MIRIAM jumps up to adjust the vents.

MIRIAM
We have to keep this going all the time. My mother has asthma.

RANDALL
My godmother had asthma. She used to brew this special tea that helped her with the spasms.

MIRIAM
Let's eat.

GITTEL
Where did she get this tea?

RANDALL
At the Chinese apothecary.

MIRIAM sits down.

GITTEL
Excuse me, Rendell, MIRIAM didn't mention it, but are you Jewish?

RANDALL
(Laughing) MIRIAM keeps telling me that I am.

GITTEL
Yes, but are your parents Jewish?

MIRIAM
(Speedily) Mom, you're not going to believe this, but RANDALL is probably a lost Jew. This is the most incredible story. Nine hundred years ago a bunch of Persian Jews settled in China in the city of Kaifeng which is a couple of hundred miles from Peking. Kaifeng was once the capitol of China and was at the end of the Silk Road. They were very successful. They built a synagogue which lasted hundreds of years. They had torahs. The emperor favored them because, because, did you know that the Chinese had no history of anti-Semitism? They actually admired these Jews because they saw that they admired their ancestors. Anyway, the Emperor favored them and gave them eight family names which they kept for generations. The family names were Zhao, Shi, Jin, Ai, Gao, Li and Zhang. And RANDALL's last name is Chang and his mother was from somewhere near Kaifeng. Isn't that
(MORE)

CONTINUED: (3)

> MIRIAM (cont'd)
> incredible? And RANDALL knows some Yiddish, don't you, RANDALL?

GITTEL's lips are drawn in a thin line.

> GITTEL
> My daughter's very educated. She reads alot. She used to read in the street. The neighbors used to tell me, wait, she'll get hit by a car. Are you Jewish, young man?

> RANDALL
> Who knows?

> GITTEL
> How were you raised?

> RANDALL
> As a Methodist.

> GITTEL
> What is that?

> RANDALL
> We went to church.

> GITTEL
> A Christian?

> RANDALL
> Yes.

> GITTEL
> Excuse me, children. (Rising) I must take a pill and lie down. I have pressure and the doctor told me to take it easy. Eat, eat. I'm just going to lie down for a few minutes.

MIRIAM and RANDALL stand.

> MIRIAM
> Can I get you anything, Mom?

> GITTEL
> Just some water and a blue pill.

EXIT GITTEL.

> MIRIAM
> I'll be right back.

73 CONTINUED: (4)

MIRIAM enters the kitchen and fills a glass with water. She fumbles with a prescription bottle and withdraws a blue pill. MIRIAM exits the kitchen and walks to GITTEL's bedroom. She knocks on the bedroom door and enters. It is dark, filled with heavy dark furniture. GITTEL is lying on the bed, a washcloth on her forehead, her shoes neatly lined up on the floor.

     MIRIAM (cont'd)
  Here, Mom. I'm sorry that you don't
  feel well.

     GITTEL
  (Hissing) Angel of Death!

              FADE OUT:

74 INT. DAY. OFFICE. ASTROPHYSICS DEPARTMENT.

Next week.

BLYTHE and DELORIS sit at their desks.

ENTER MIRIAM.

MIRIAM is pale. She sits clumsily at her desk. The drawer stays shut.

     BLYTHE
  How is she?

     MIRIAM
  She had a stroke.

     DELORIS
  Jeez.

     BLYTHE
  Is she going to be alright?

     MIRIAM
  She can't speak and she's blind in one
  eye. She may regain some speech with
  therapy.

     BLYTHE
  Is she still in the hospital?

     MIRIAM
  Yes. (Rubbing her forehead) They have
  her on blood thinners to prevent
  another stroke.

BLYTHE
I guess this sort of changes everything.

MIRIAM
(Smiling wanly) Not really. It's always been like this.

DELORIS
What do you mean?

MIRIAM
It's too hard to explain.

DELORIS
What about your plans?

MIRIAM
Aft gang astray.

BLYTHE
What?

DELORIS
Oh, MIRIAM's quoting some Scottish poet.

BLYTHE
What are you going to do? DELORIS and I are leaving at the end of the week. This was just a temporary job.

MIRIAM
I'm not going anywhere. I spoke with Professor Norton. He's keeping me on.

BLYTHE
What about RANDALL?

MIRIAM
He's going to Cambridge. He's taking six months at Harvard.

BLYTHE
And you? What about law school?

MIRIAM rises and walks to the dusty, grime streaked window overlooking the university quadrangle.

MIRIAM
I have to take care of my mother. Do you know of anyone that would want to
(MORE)

74   CONTINUED: (2)

                    MIRIAM (cont'd)
            buy a used Chevy Vega? It gets great
            mileage.

                                        FADE OUT:

75   EXT. DAY. OFFICE BUILDING.   75

    MIRIAM is walking down Broadway. It is overcast and
    raining. She stands under a store canopy and looks up at
    the sky. Suddenly, a car pulls up to the curb. The
    passenger door swings open. It being driven by RANDALL.

                    RANDALL
            Get in.

                    MIRIAM
            I can't.

                    RANDALL
            I said to get in. Please.

    MIRIAM walks toward the vehicle and enters. The windows
    are steamed up. RANDALL drives on.

                    RANDALL (cont'd)
            I called you at home, at the office
            and at the hospital. What's going on?

                    MIRIAM
            Please don't do this.

                    RANDALL
            I thought you were stronger than this.

                    MIRIAM
            You were wrong. You don't understand,
            I have this, the whole weight of
            history imploding within me.

                    RANDALL
            You've been reading too many of your
            project proposals.

                    MIRIAM
            (Laughing) I haven't laughed in a
            while.

                    RANDALL
            How's your mother?

                    MIRIAM
            There's some progress.

CONTINUED:

> RANDALL
> Listen, you're not the only one that has this burden. My family went through a Holocaust of their own.

> MIRIAM
> It's not the same thing.

> RANDALL
> Maybe it was worse. Our own people tried to destroy us.

The windshield wipers continue to beat as MIRIAM and RANDALL fall silent.

> MIRIAM
> I don't want to be responsible for killing her!

> RANDALL
> I understand. MIRIAM. I'm going to Cambridge and you're coming with me.

> MIRIAM
> No! I can't. It's impossible.

> RANDALL
> We'll take her with us.

> MIRIAM
> What?

> RANDALL
> My friend, Simon. I told you about him. His dad owns a chain of nursing homes. I've spoken with him. We'll place her there until her rehab is finished and then, we'll take it day by day.

> MIRIAM
> You'd do this for me? You'd take responsibility for someone who is half-crazed?

> RANDALL
> You can take medication.

> MIRIAM
> I meant my mother.

> RANDALL
> I'll be the best eiden she ever had.

CONTINUED: (2)

                MIRIAM
        What's that?

                RANDALL
        Son-in-law.

                MIRIAM
        You're unbelievable.

                RANDALL
        I'll even learn to eat kosher food.

                MIRIAM
        No more won-tons?

RANDALL leans over and kisses MIRIAM as car horns honk loudly.

                RANDALL
        We just sealed the deal.

                MIRIAM
        Do you really think we can do this?

                RANDALL
        Vu den?

                MIRIAM
        All right that's enough. This isn't
        right. I don't know anything about
        your culture.

                RANDALL
        You're my culture.

                MIRIAM
        All I know is that this is supposed to
        be the Year of the what--the Dragon?
        Isn't it?

                RANDALL
        We'll have to ask my Aunt Mildred.

                MIRIAM
        You have an Aunt Mildred? Tell me, is
        she married to an Uncle Harry?

                RANDALL
        As a matter of fact, his name is
        Herbert.

CONTINUED: (3)

> MIRIAM
> I bet he was named after Herbert Hoover.

> RANDALL
> You've met him?

> MIRIAM
> I don't think so. We don't meet too many Republicans in Brooklyn.

> RANDALL
> Well, Mrs. Chang, where to?

> MIRIAM
> Mrs. Chang? Mrs. Chang. It has a certain ring to it. But isn't this all about choice? Shouldn't women be able to keep their maiden names if they want to?

> RANDALL
> I think--

> MIRIAM
> Well, I do. If--if you agree.
> (Smiling)

FADE OUT:

THE END

Made in United States
Orlando, FL
18 March 2025